# Cookin

## with

# WILL ROGERS

## By Sharon and Gene McFall

*cookbook resources*

PUBLISHED BY COOKBOOK RESOURCES, LLC

## ACKNOWLEDGEMENTS

My most heartfelt thanks to:

My husband and co-author, Gene McFall, whose inspiration and assistance made *Cookin' With Will Rogers* not just another cookbook, but something special.

Jim and Judy Rogers for their comments, encouragement and recipes.

Clem and Donna McSpadden for their help and family recipes.

The many Will Rogers fans who contributed their favorite recipes.

The Will Rogers Memorial and their expert staff who provided pictures, quotes, stories and other extensive resources to make this book accurate as well as entertaining.

Cookbook Resources who heard our ideas and developed them into a remarkable book.

—Sharon McFall

Book Development, Sheryn R. Jones
Book Design, Barbara Jezek
Photography, Will Rogers Museum

First Printing 2000
Second Printing 2001

ISBN  0-9677932-1-1
Library of Congress Card Catalog #00-111759

Developed, Edited, Manufactured and Published in the United States of America by
Cookbook Resources, LLC
541 Doubletree Drive
Highland Village, Texas  75077
www.cookbookresources.com

*cookbook*
*resources*

# FOREWORD

## By Jim Rogers – Will Rogers' son

When Sharon and Gene McFall asked me if I would write an introduction for their new Revised Edition of "Cookin' with Will Rogers" I said that I would be very proud to do so. As I looked through the book I found it full of recipes of the kind of dishes I grew up eating. Both Dad and Mother's people were Southerners and they were raised on what I called "Midwestern Southern Cooking."

I have known Gene McFall for a lot of years as he has been doing his one man show, THE WITTY WORLD OF WILL ROGERS for about 18 years, and has studied Dad's life and his writings and is a far greater authority than I. Traveling as he does with his show, Gene and Sharon have made many friends and collected a great many recipes of the kind of meals Dad would have enjoyed.

Now, Dad didn't take a back seat to anyone when it came to eating and he sure liked that old-time style of cooking – lots of meat and potatoes and beans and greens – but as a chef he was kind of at the bottom of the class. In this book you will find a host of those "old time tasty creations" as well as many more of today's modern ones. I am sure you will find Sharon's "Helpful Hints:" and other cooking information to be a great help in turning a written recipe into a gastronomic experience.

# CONTENTS

# ABOUT THE AUTHORS

## Sharon McFall

Sharon is a native of Des Moines, Iowa. For the past 10 years she has traveled extensively in the United States and around the world. In her varied experiences she has coordinated major seminars in the Midwest for working women, owned and operated a restaurant and concessions at a major country music center, designed and developed gift shops and women's apparel shops in important tourist areas and was vice-president of operations for a dinner theatre.

She is the mother of four children and enjoys spoiling her two granddaughters and two grandsons. When not collecting recipes and writing cookbooks, Sharon promotes and books her husband, Gene McFall's one-man show, WITTY WORLD OF WILL ROGERS. She currently resides in Will Rogers' hometown of Claremore, Oklahoma.

## Gene McFall

Around the globe and across the nation into 45 states, Gene McFall has performed his prize-winning role of Will Rogers since 1982. Other than James Whitmore, McFall was the first person to perform WILL ROGERS' USA. Drawing from the archives of the Will Rogers Memorial at Claremore, Oklahoma, Gene wrote his own one-man show, WITTY WORLD OF WILL ROGERS, in 1989. Cast as Will Rogers, he was major player in the public television production, OKLAHOMA PASSAGE.

In his classic Will Rogers' role, Gene McFall drew praise in performances before Will Rogers' own children, President George Bush, Supreme Court Justice Byron White, UN Ambassador Jean Kirkpatrick, scores of U. S. Senators and Congressmen, Governors and state lawmakers in stage productions and during shows at conventions. Gene is the radio and television spokesman for the Oklahoma Credit Union League.

In a special staff role, Gene keeps Will Rogers alive to the school children of Oklahoma in a special program sponsored by the Will Rogers Memorial Commission, the Will Rogers Heritage Trust, Inc. and the Oklahoma Legislature.

# INTRODUCTION

This cookbook is dedicated to one of the best known and most beloved Americans this country has ever had, Oklahoma's favorite son, the cowboy humorist/philosopher, William Penn Adair Rogers. Although he was killed in 1935, his memory lives on and his quotes are as timely today as when he wrote or said them.

You may ask, "Why a cookbook to Will Rogers?  Was he a cook?" Will's culinary efforts were very simple, an ever-present pot of beans, a pone of cornbread and possibly a pot of chili. He liked to cook whenever he had the time, but he was more of a consumer than a producer. He loved good food, but was a meat and potatoes man, preferring simple nourishing fare.

On his lecture tour he would often try to find a good chili parlor, eat a couple of bowls before his talk, so he could avoid the food on what he called "the rubber chicken circuit".

The things Will Rogers stood for are love of home and family, affection for his fellow man as immortalized in his most famous quote, "I never met a man I didn't like", love of America and his native state of Oklahoma, his untiring efforts to help his fellow man, his generosity with both his time and his money and the exemplary life he led. These are a few of the reasons to honor his in this book.

Some of the recipes are from Will Rogers and the Rogers family. Others are from the time period in which he was the most popular enter-tainer in the world. Friends and family of the author have contributed their favorite recipes. Ease of preparation and simplicity of ingredients have been major factors in selecting recipes for this collection—recipes Will Rogers would have enjoyed.

**Will Rogers in** *Handy Andy.*

# DOG IRON RANCH

## Will Rogers' Birthplace — Dog Iron Ranch
## Oologah, Oklahoma

Will Rogers was born in 1879 in one of the four original log rooms at his parent's ranch at Oologah, Oklahoma. He joked that his mother wanted him to be able to say that he had been born in a log cabin so he might become President of the United States.

The "White House on the Verdigris" was a favorite stopover for prominent people and was a place of government meetings, court actions, religious and social gatherings.

When Will's mother died, Clem moved to Claremore and the house fell into disuse. Will eventually bought out his sisters' shares in the ranch. In 1927 he convinced his nephew, Herb McSpadden to move into the house and manage the ranch.

In 1959 when Lake Oologah was going to inundate the house site, the house was donated to the state of Oklahoma. It was moved to higher ground and was eventually placed under the management of the Will Rogers Memorial Commission.

It is now an 1879 "Living History Ranch", complete with a herd of longhorn cattle, goats, sheep, horses, peacocks and other farm animals of that era with a barn built by the Amish with wooden peg construction.

The ranch and house are open to the public 365 days a year. A tremendous view overlooking Lake Oologah, picnic facilities, overnight camper hookups, a grass landing strip and an air-conditioned meeting room in the barn make it a popular tourist stop.

# WILL ROGERS
## November 4, 1879 – August 15, 1935

Will Rogers was of Cherokee Indian ancestry. His family saw that relocation was inevitable and moved from Georgia to Indian Territory (what is now eastern Oklahoma) before the forced removal of the Indians over the Trail of Tears. Will's father, Clement Vann Rogers, met Mary America Schrimsher, the daughter of a prominent Cherokee plantation family, at school in Tahlequah. They were both approximately one-fourth Cherokee. They married and started the first ranch in the Cooweescoowee district of Indian Territory.

They were doing fine until the advent of the Civil War. Clem, like many of the Cherokee, fought for the Confederacy. He became a captain under the Cherokee General Stand Waite. When Clem returned from the war, his livestock had been run off and his buildings torn down. He moved a few miles east to the Verdigris River near Oologah and started all over.

He drove longhorn cattle from Texas to his ranch, fattened them on the rich bluestem prairie grass and then drove them to the railhead in Kansas. His ranch at one time encompassed over 60,000 acres, none of which he owned, because the Indian lands were held in common ownership. They built an impressive home which became a stopover for many prominent people visiting that part of Indian Territory. Clem was influential in affairs of the Cherokee Nation and later was a delegate to the statehood convention when Oklahoma became a state. Rogers County, Oklahoma is named for Clem Rogers.

Will was the eighth and last child born to Clem and Mary. He was born November 4, 1879. Three children died in infancy and his brother died when Will was three years old. He was raised with three older sisters and was the youngest and only boy.

**Will Rogers, California Governor James Ralph, Jr., and W. K. Kellog at the Kellog Arabian Horse Ranch, May 17, 1932.**

Will attended several different schools, doing very well in subjects in which he was interested, but spent a minimum of time on those which bored him. He had an excellent memory, could glance through an assignment on the way to class and retain enough to get him by. He quit his last school, Kemper Military Academy in Booneville, Missouri, near the end of his junior year in high school. (He often joked about never getting past fourth grade McGuffey's reader.) He did not like the strict regime at Kemper and all he wanted to do was be a cowboy, so he needed no further education.

After a stint as a cowboy in the panhandle of Texas and a try at running the home ranch, he and a friend, Dick Paris, headed for the wide open spaces of Argentina. Finding superbly skilled gauchos with whom it was hard to compete, $7.00 a month cowboy wages and dwindling funds in Argentina, Dick Paris returned home and Will Rogers got a job as a cattle tender on a boat loaded with cattle headed for South Africa.

In South Africa Will needed a job. He auditioned for Texas Jack who was there with his Wild West Show. Using roping skills he had developed on his father's ranch under the guidance of Uncle Dan Walker, Will was hired to perform as "The Cherokee Kid, World's Champion Lassoer".

After his return to the United States, he met Betty Blake from Rogers, Arkansas, who was visiting her sister in Oologah. They started a courtship that was conducted mainly by correspondence over several years, seeing each other only on infrequent occasions.

After an extended courtship, Will convinced Betty to marry him. She agreed, but with the stipulation that she would travel with Will for the duration of a three months tour, then he would quit show business, come back to Oklahoma, get a job and start working for a living. Before the tour was over, Will was offered another booking for much more money. Betty agreed that he should take the booking. Will never came back to Oklahoma to "work for a living". Instead he became the most popular and highest paid entertainer in the world.

Will became a star in the biggest stage show of his day, the Ziegfeld Follies. He changed his act and started his witty commentary on the current events of the day. "Well, all I know is what I read in the papers."

Then he started writing for the newspapers. He had a little one-paragraph column in which he poked fun at Congress, politicians, government, big business, lawyers, doctors and anyone else he thought was doing something foolish. It was carried in over 500 newspapers throughout the country and read by at least one-third of the nation. He also had a much longer weekly column that was carried in about the same number of papers.

He became the first radio personality and was on the first coast-to-coast radio broadcast. He was the highest paid man in radio. Preachers

**Will Rogers in the silent film, _The Cake Eater._**

complained about his Sunday night radio show. They said that people were staying home from church to listen to his radio broadcasts. Movie houses stopped their film and rolled a radio out on stage for people to listen to his show.

The movies were becoming our most popular form of entertainment, so naturally they wanted Will Rogers. He made 50 silent films, then made 21 "talkies". He never won an Academy Award, but each of his movies made from 1930 to 1935 earned Fox Studios at least one million dollars. In 1933-34-35 he was the number one male box office attraction in movies. He was the top box office attraction in 1934. Shirley Temple beat him out in 1935. Will said there were only two things he claimed for himself in the movies: "One, I'm the ugliest man in them. Second, I'm the only guy that's still got the same wife he started out with."

**Will Rogers with Mr. and Mrs. Babe Ruth in Boston in the 1920's.**

Will and Betty had four children: Will, Jr., Mary, Jim and Freddie. Freddie died at the age of 23 months. Mary died in 1989 and Will, Jr. passed away in 1993. Jim is a retired rancher living in Bakersfield, California.

Betty stayed home and raised the family while Will traveled the world, but he was a very good father when he was home. Whenever possible Will would take Betty or the children with him on his travels.

Will was an aviation enthusiast and flew whenever and wherever he could. He was a friend with all the prominent aviators of his day. He flew to scenes of disaster to render whatever assistance he could, often beating the Red Cross to the scene. He was the only private citizen to have special permission to fly across the country in mail planes.

Will Rogers was friends with and performed for presidents, kings, queens and heads of state. Franklin D. Roosevelt especially valued Will's friendship and his understanding of what the average citizen was thinking, both in this country and abroad.

Will Rogers was killed in a plane crash with Wiley Post near Point Barrow, Alaska on August 15, 1935. Great national grief followed his death. For many Americans it was like losing a member of the family.

## BETTY BLAKE ROGERS (Wife of Will Rogers)
## 1879 – 1944

The daughter of Amelia J. Crowder and James Wyethy Blake, Betty Blake Rogers was born September 9, 1879 at Rogers, Benton County, Arkansas. She had six sisters and one half-sister.

Betty first met Will Rogers in 1899 while visiting her sister in Oologah, Oklahoma. They had a lengthy courtship, mainly by correspondence and were married in 1908 after Will had become successful enough to support a family. They were both 29 years old.

Will's true success, greatness and fame occurred during the couple's ensuing 26-year marriage. Often described as modest and self-effacing, Betty Rogers stayed away from publicity and tried to remain in the background, but she played a major role behind the scenes and assumed multiple responsibilities as mother, homemaker and manager of the family's financial affairs.

Betty helped establish the first church in Beverly Hills, California and was active in charity work, including the Red Cross. She never told jokes, but her eyes sparkled in response to humor. She was unabashed about her love for her husband and her children and radiated appreciation at any mention of her family.

Following Will Rogers' death, Betty became more public as a family spokesperson and more actively managed family affairs, consulting with her three children who remained close friends throughout long lives.

Betty Rogers wrote a memoir of her husband that was serialized in "The Saturday Evening Post". It then was published as a biography by the University of Oklahoma Press and remained a brisk seller for more than 60 years.

# JAMES BLAKE ROGERS

Jim was born in New York City July 25, 1915, the third child of Will and Betty Rogers, while his father was a star in the Ziegfeld Follies. Will moved his family to Beverly Hills, California to work in motion pictures and Jim grew up there.

Jimmy's first experience in the movies came as appearances in three of Will Rogers' feature films. He did not make a career as an actor, but he was a cowboy in three Hopalong Cassidy westerns, made three comedy cowboy movies with Noah Beery, Jr. and made training films for the Army with Rod Cameron.

Jim Rogers was at one time editor-publisher of the family newspaper, "The Beverly Hills Citizen". He also was a writer correspondent in the Marine Corps during the latter part of World War II.

He and his late wife, Astrea, had three children: Kem Rogers, a cattleman, Chuck Rogers, a professional polo player, and Betty Brandin.

Jim Rogers is closely involved with the Will Rogers State Park, the home, ranch and polo grounds that were donated to the state of California upon his mother's death. He is the family representative on the Will Rogers Memorial Commission of Oklahoma and as an active participant and consultant has helped make the Will Rogers Memorial Museum the world-class attraction it is today.

Jim may not look as much like his father as did Will, Jr. but his friendly, gregarious personality and great sense of humor are reminiscent of his famous dad.

Jim and his wife, Judy Braun, own a stable and are active horse people in Bakersfield, California.

# WILL ROGERS MUSEUM

In 1911 Will Rogers bought 20 acres of land overlooking the city of Claremore for $400 per acre. He said that when he retired he might build a house and live there part of the time.

When he was killed there was great interest nationally in building a memorial to him. His wife Betty offered to donate the land in Claremore for that purpose. The Oklahoma State Legislature appropriated $200,000 and with the use of some private donations, the Will Rogers Memorial was dedicated on November 4, 1938.

Will Rogers' body was originally interred in Glendale, California, but in 1944 he was moved to a family crypt on the Museum grounds. Will, his wife Betty, their son Freddie, daughter Mary and daughter-in-law Astrea now rest in the tomb.

In 1982 a major expansion included a vault, a theatre and more exhibit space.

The Will Rogers Memorial Museum in Claremore, Oklahoma houses memorabilia, artifacts, art works, a research library with Will's writings and papers, recordings and movies, all preserving the life and career of this great American. It is one of the top tourist attractions in Oklahoma and receives many thousands of visitors annually from all over the world.

# MUNCHIES AND GULLEY WASHERS

## [appetizers]

# WILL ROGERS—THE MAN

**Will Rogers spins
a big loop on
horseback.**

### Will Rogers . . .

. . . was very generous with his time and money,
and he did it without a lot of fanfare. During
World War I he donated $100 a week to the Red
Cross and $100 a week to the Salvation Army for
the duration of the war. He was not making a
spectacular salary at the time. It was said that
he often beat the Red Cross to the scene of a
disaster. Nicaragua issued a series of postage
stamps in his honor for his humanitarian efforts
after an earthquake there. In the late 20s when

flooding had devastated the farmers along the Mississippi River, Will hired a group of entertainers, paid their salaries and expenses, and did a series of concerts to benefit the farmers. When the drought hit in the early 30s, he did the same thing again, raising considerable sums to aid the farmers.

. . . attended hundreds of banquets both here and abroad. He sampled the wares of the world's most celebrated chefs, but his taste in food remained simple. There was nothing he would rather eat than beans, especially navy beans. He was a connoisseur of beans—a bean man all the way.

**Will Rogers at his Beverly Hills home in 1927-28**

. . . roping skills began under the guidance of Uncle Dan Walker, who worked on the Rogers ranch. His passion for fancy rope tricks and rope spinning was inspired when he and his father attended the 1893 Chicago World's Fair. There he saw a spectacular performance by a Mexican, Vincente Oropeza, billed as "the greatest roper in the world." Roping was always an important part of Will's life. He originated many rope

**Will Rogers, Akdar Temple Shriner**

**Will Rogers, America's most accomplished human document. One third humor. One third humanitarian. One third heart.**

*—Damon Runyon*

tricks, some of which have never been duplicated.

. . . was the best known American all over the world, and the best loved private citizen in the United States.

. . . felt that money was for spending and giving. He brought unlimited happiness and comfort for others. When he would go to New York after he became very successful, he would fill his pockets with one-dollar bills. Every actor Will met on the streets would want to tell Will where they had worked together. None ever went away empty handed.

. . . is one of the most quoted Americans we have ever had. If you don't know who said a witty saying, attribute it to either Mark Twain or Will Rogers—you usually have a 50-50 chance of being right.

. . . lessons of life, visions of humanity and kind spirit more powerfully were formed into wit,

**I work with gum and grin and lariat
To entertain the proletariat.
And with my Oklahomey wit
I brighten up the earth a bit.**

*—Ogden Nash, Poet sums up Will Rogers*

jokes and observations that bespoke great human dimensions.

. . . masterful roping tricks would enter the *Guinness Book of Records* while his words about brotherhood and human kindness would be written across the heart of humanity.

. . . favorite targets were the biggest politicians. He spared neither side. To heap scorn on the system, he proclaimed himself a prank candidate for president pledging only to resign if elected.

**A painting of Will Rogers by Howard Chandler Christie which hangs in the Will Rogers State Park in California**

. . . produced, directed and starred in his memorable *Ropin Fool* film that captured his skills as a roper, writer and slow motion cinema innovator.

## WILL'S STUFFED LA SHRIMP
### A recipe of Will Rogers

*1 cup shrimp, shredded*
*¼ cup minced celery*
*2 tablespoon mayonnaise*
*2 to 3 celery ribs*

Mix shrimp with minced celery. Add mayonnaise and stuff ribs of celery with mixture.

Ω

## DIPPED WINGS

*¾ cup teriyaki sauce*
*3 cloves garlic, minced*
*2½ pounds chicken wings*

**"You know I had Indian blood in me. Had just enough white blood to make my honesty questionable."**

— *Will Rogers*

In a 9 x 13-inch pan, stir together teriyaki sauce and 3 cloves garlic. Add wings and stir until evenly coated. Spread wings on a sheet pan. Bake at 475° for 30 to 40 minutes. Serve with peanut sauce. Makes 4 to 5 servings.

**Peanut Sauce:**

*¼ cup teriyaki sauce*
*1 garlic clove, minced*
*¼ cup peanut butter*
*1 tablespoon rice vinegar*

Put teriyaki sauce, garlic, peanut butter and rice vinegar into food processor. Whirl until smooth. Pour into small bowl and dip wings in cooled peanut sauce.

## CROWNED MUSHROOMS

2 (6-ounce) cans mushroom crowns
3 slices bacon
1 thin slice onion
Dash Worcestershire sauce
½ teaspoon salt
1 slice bread
3 tablespoons grated Parmesan cheese

Hollow out mushrooms and reserve ¼ cup of pieces. Crisp cook bacon, drain and reserve drippings. Cook onion in drippings until tender. Put onion, bacon, reserved mushrooms, Worcestershire sauce, salt and slice bread torn in pieces, in with bacon drippings. Blend until well mixed. Put mushrooms on baking pan and pile mixture in crowns. Top with cheese. Broil 3 to 4 inches from heat until golden. Makes 30.

Ω

## BAKED POTATO SKINS

4 potatoes
4 teaspoons butter, divided
2 tablespoons grated Parmesan cheese
1 cup grated cheddar cheese
Salt
Pepper

Bake potatoes at 400° or microwave until done. Immediately slice each potato in half lengthwise. With a spoon scoop out most of the potato, rub 1 teaspoon of butter in each potato. Sprinkle skins with Parmesan cheese and cheddar cheese. Salt and pepper to taste. Broil until cheese has browned lightly.

"Popularity is the easiest thing in the world to gain and the hardest to hold."

— Will Rogers

[23]

## CHILIES CON QUESO

*1 (16-ounce) jar cheese spread*
*1 (4-ounce) can chopped, green chilies, drained*
*1 (2-ounce) jar diced pimientos, drained*

Heat all ingredients over low heat, stirring constantly until cheese is melted, about 2 minutes. Pour into fondue pot or chafing dish. Keep warm over low heat. Serve with tortilla chips or bite-size fresh vegetables. Makes 2 cups. *(Judy Krause)*

∩

## HOT CHEDDAR CHEESE WEDGES

**"We may elevate ourselves, but we should never reach so high that we would ever forget those who helped us get there."**

— *Will Rogers*

*¼ cup butter, softened*
*1 pound cheddar cheese spread*
*¼ teaspoon cracked pepper*
*½ teaspoon onion salt*
*¼ teaspoon garlic powder*
*¾ teaspoon Worcestershire sauce*
*5 English muffins*

Cream butter, cheese spread, pepper, onion, salt and garlic powder until well blended. Add Worcestershire sauce. Spread generously on split English muffins. The cheese should be ¼ inch thick. Bake at 300° for 7 minutes. Cut in quarters and serve on a hot plate.

∩

## TACO NACHO DIP

*1 pound ground beef, browned*
*2 cups shredded colby cheese*
*1 (16-ounce) can refried beans*
*1 package taco seasoning*

Combine all ingredients in saucepan. Cook on low heat, stir until cheese has melted. Serve with chips.

## TACO MUNCHIES

1 pound skinless, boneless, chicken breasts
1 package taco seasoning mix
1 cup crushed tortilla chips
1 cup butter, melted
1 (8-ounce) jar salsa

Cut chicken into bite-size pieces. Combine taco seasoning and tortilla chips. Spear each chicken piece
with toothpick, dip in butter and roll each in taco/tor-
tilla crumbs mixture. Place on baking sheet. Bake at
350° for 20 to 30 minutes. Serve with salsa.

∩

## MOM'S DYNAMITE DIP

1 (16-ounce) container sour cream
1 envelope Lipton beefy onion soup mix
2 to 3 tablespoons chopped jalapenos

Mix together all ingredients. (Kathy Jekel)

∩

## LAND RUN DIP

2 large tomatoes, chopped
4 green onions, chopped
1 (4-ounce) can chopped green chilies
1 (4-ounce) can chopped olives
3 teaspoons olive oil
1 teaspoon garlic salt
1 tablespoon vinegar

Place tomatoes and green onions in bowl. Drain
green chilies and olives and add to bowl. Add olive
oil, garlic salt and vinegar and mix well. Cover and
cool at least 2 hours.

"I am just an
ol' country
boy in a big
town tryin to
get along. I
have been
eatin pretty
regular and
the reason is
because I
have stayed
an ol'
country
boy."

— Will Rogers

## CHEROKEE RUN REFRIED BEAN DIP

*1 (15-ounce) can refried beans*
*1 (8-ounce) container sour cream*
*1 package taco seasoning*
*1 (4-ounce) can chopped green chilies*
*2 to 3 green onions, chopped*
*8 to 10 ounces processed cheese, cubed*

**No man is
great if he
thinks he is.**

— *Will Rogers*

In glass microwave dish combine all ingredients. Carefully microwave until cheese is melted and stir often. Serve with chips.

∩

## MULESKINNER'S BEEF DIP

*1 (8-ounce) package cream cheese, softened*
*1 cup sour cream*
*3 ounces dried beef, finely chopped*
*1 tablespoon vinegar*
*1½ tablespoons minced onion*
*½ teaspoon garlic powder*
*Pepper*

Combine all ingredients and mix well. Put in 1-quart baking dish. Bake at 375° for 30 minutes. Serve with raw vegetables or crackers. Makes 2 cups.

∩

## OYSTER DIP DELIGHT

*1 (3-ounce) can smoked oysters, undrained*
*2 (8-ounce) packages cream cheese, softened*
*1 teaspoon Worcestershire sauce*
*2 teaspoons lemon juice*
*1 cup sour cream*

Blend oysters and cheese. Add other ingredients and mix well. Serve with corn or potato chips. Makes 12-14 servings.

## CRAB DIP TEASERS

1 (8-ounce) package cream cheese
2 green onions, diced
3 tablespoons mayonnaise
2 teaspoons lemon juice
1 teaspoon Worcestershire sauce
1 (6-oz) can crabmeat, drained

In a 1-quart serving dish, microwave the cream cheese at 50% (medium) for 1½ to 3 minutes. Blend in the onions, mayonnaise, lemon juice and Worcestershire sauce. Stir in crab-meat. Microwave at 50% (medium) for 5 minutes stirring after every minute of cooking time. Serve with bread sticks, Melba toast or potato chips.

Ω

## AVOCADO WITH CRAB DIP

1 large avocado, halved, cubed
1 tablespoon lemon juice
1 thin slice onion, minced
1 teaspoon Worcestershire sauce
1 (8-ounce) package cream cheese, softened
¼ cup sour cream
¼ teaspoon salt
1 (7½-ounce) can chopped, green chilies
Crabmeat, picked

Put avocado, lemon juice, onion and Worcestershire in bowl and blend until smooth. Add cream cheese, sour cream and salt to mixture. Blend until smooth and stir in green chilies and crabmeat. Chill well and serve with assorted crackers.

I'm
practically
world
famous for
my
ignorance.
— Will Rogers

## DELICIOUS MEXIE DIP

*1 (8-ounce) Mexican Velveeta cheese*
*1 (15-ounce) can no bean chili*

Put Mexican cheese and chili in saucepan on low heat. Stir until cheese has melted. Serve with taco chips.

∩

## CHILI CON QUESO DIP

*1 cup shredded cheddar cheese*
*1 cup shredded Jack cheese*
*½ tablespoon cornstarch*
*3 tablespoons oil*
*½ cup chopped onion*
*1 clove garlic, minced*
*1 teaspoon chili powder*
*1 (14½-ounce) can whole tomatoes,*
  *drained, chopped*
*1 (4-ounce) can chopped green chilies, drained*

In bowl, toss together all cheeses and cornstarch until evenly coated. Heat oil in skillet and add onion, garlic, chili powder, tomatoes and green chilies. Stirring frequently, bring to a boil. Reduce heat and simmer 10 minutes. Gradually stir in cheese. When melted, take off heat and serve with taco chips.

## PEPPER BOWL DIP

1 (7-ounce) jar sweet roasted red peppers,
  drained, chopped
1 garlic clove, minced
1 tablespoon fresh basil leaves, thinly sliced
1 cup sour cream
1 cup mayonnaise
½ teaspoon Worcestershire sauce
1 teaspoon salt
1 large green or red pepper

Mix all ingredients except green or red peppers. Cut off top of green pepper, remove membranes and seeds and fill with dip. Use with assorted fresh vegetables.

∩

## SPINACH SURPRISE DIP

1 (10-ounce) package frozen spinach
2 cups mayonnaise
½ cup chopped, green onions
1 cup finely chopped parsley

Cook spinach according to package directions. Drain well and mash to drain more. Mix with other ingredients and let set 24 hours in refrigerator. Makes 3 cups. Great with vegetables.

Only one amusement line I haven't been in and that's the United States Senate. And I'm not gonna try that. I still got some pride left.

— Will Rogers

## FIRESIDE SHRIMP COCKTAIL SAUCE

¾ cup chili sauce
2 tablespoons lemon juice
2 tablespoons horseradish
2 teaspoons Worcestershire sauce
1 teaspoon grated onion
Dash Tabasco sauce
Salt
Cooked shrimp

Combine all ingredients except salt. Add salt to taste and mix well. Served with cooked shrimp.

Ω

## GUACAMOLE

2 avocados, peeled
½ onion, minced
1 tablespoon vinegar
Salt
Pepper
Chopped green chili pepper
1 ripe tomato, peeled, finely chopped

**My motto is, Save America first.**

— Will Rogers

In bowl beat avocados, onion, vinegar, salt, pepper and green chili pepper with electric mixer on medium speed until smooth. Fold tomato into mixture. Serve with chips.

## ROUTE 66 DIP

3 eggs, beaten
2 tablespoons vinegar
2 tablespoons sugar
1 tablespoon butter
1 (8–ounce) package cream cheese, softened
1 green bell pepper, chopped
1 red pepper, chopped
1 small onion, chopped
2 drops Tabasco
¼ teaspoon salt

Cook eggs, vinegar and sugar in saucepan on low heat for 3 minutes, stirring constantly. Add butter and cream cheese and stir until melted. Remove from heat and beat with mixer until smooth. Add remaining ingredients and mix well. Serve with Frito chips.

> Call me a 'rube and a hick' but I'd a lot rather be the man who bought the Brooklyn Bridge than the man who sold it.
>
> — *Will Rogers*

Ω

## LOW-FAT HERB DIP

1 envelope Italian or garlic and herb salad
    dressing mix
1 cup low-fat yogurt
2 tablespoons finely chopped green onions

Combine all ingredients in a bowl and mix well. Chill at least 1 hour. Makes 2 cups.

Ω

## DELIGHTFUL FRUIT DIP

1 cup crushed macaroon cookies
1 cup sour cream
2 tablespoons brown sugar

In large bowl mix together all ingredients. Serve with fruit.

**[31]**

## PEACH CLOUDS

*1 cup whipped topping*
*1 (8-ounce) container peach yogurt*
*½ cup finely chopped peaches*

Mix all ingredients in small bowl. Serve as a dip with fresh fruit.

## LOW-FAT YOGURT DIP

*1 envelope Italian or garlic salad dressing mix*
*1 cup low-fat yogurt*
*2 tablespoons finely chopped green onions*

Combine all ingredients in bowl and mix well. Chill at least 1 hour. Great with vegetables. Makes 2 cups.

## OLD WEST STYLE DIP

*1 (8-ounce) package cream cheese, softened*
*1 (15-ounce) can no-bean chili*
*3 tablespoons taco sauce*
*1 cup grated cheddar cheese*

Spread cream cheese on bottom of pie plate. Cover with chili, taco sauce and grated cheese. Bake for 30 minutes at 300°. Serve with tortilla chips.

## PICKLE ROLLS

*1 package cooked ham slices*
*1 (8-ounce) package cream cheese, softened*
*8 pickles*

Spread ham with cream cheese. Wrap each slice around a pickle and chill. Slice each pickle roll and put on plate.

## HAM-CHEESE LOG

1 cup shredded cheddar cheese, softened
1 (8-ounce) package cream cheese, softened
1 (4½-ounce) can deviled ham
½ cup pitted, chopped ripe olives
½ cup chopped pecans

Have cheddar cheese at room temperature and in small mixing bowl blend together cheddar cheese and cream cheese. Beat in deviled ham, stir in olives and chill. Shape into 2 (8-inch) logs and roll in pecans. Great holiday fare.

Ω

## HAM-IT-UP BALL

1 (8-ounce) package cream cheese, softened
¼ cup salad dressing
2 cups cooked, ground ham
2 tablespoons chopped parsley
1 teaspoon minced onion
¼ teaspoon dry mustard
¼ teaspoon hot pepper sauce
½ cup chopped peanuts

Beat cream cheese and salad dressing until smooth. Mix ham, parsley, onion, mustard and hot pepper sauce. Pour into cream cheese mixture and mix well. Cover; chill several hours. Form into ball, roll into nuts. Serve with crackers.

**There has never been anything invented yet, including war, that a man would enter into that a woman wouldn't too.**

—Will Rogers

## CHEESE BALL

1 (8-ounce) package cream cheese, softened
1 green onion, chopped
1 (3-ounce) package dried beef, finely chopped
1 tablespoon Worcestershire sauce
½ cup finely chopped pecans

Cream all ingredients except pecans. Cover and chill. Shape into a ball. Cover with pecans. Serve with crackers. (Dr. Dick Reasoner)

∩

## SAUSAGE BALLS

1 pound sharp cheese, grated
1 pound sausage
3 cups biscuit mix

Heat oven to 350°. Bring cheese to room temperature and mix with sausage and biscuit mix, using fork. Shape into 1-inch balls and place on ungreased, baking sheet. Bake 12 to 15 minutes. Serve hot or cold. Great for a party. Makes about 40.

∩

## CHEESE TUNA BALLS

2 (6-ounce) cans tuna, drained
1 (8-ounce) package cream cheese, softened
1 tablespoon lemon juice
2 tablespoons grated onion
½ cup chopped nuts

Mix all ingredients except nuts. Form into ball and roll in nuts. Serve with crackers.

**Great artists say that the most beautiful thing in the world is a little baby. Well, the next is an old lady, for every wrinkle is a picture.**

—*Will Rogers*

[34]

## GREAT FAST & EASY CHEESE BALL

Office of Secretary of State, Oklahoma, Kathy Jekel

2 (8-ounce) packages cream cheese, softened
1 tablespoon beef bouillon
1 tablespoon chicken bouillon
¼ teaspoon liquid smoke
¼ teaspoon garlic salt
1 tablespoon Worcestershire sauce
3 green onions, finely chopped
½ cup finely chopped walnuts, divided

Mix all ingredients with ¼ cup walnuts. Mash with a spoon to push the flavor into the cheese. Form into a ball and roll in remaining nuts.

Can be served right away, but better if sets overnight in refrigerator. Serve with your favorite cracker or Wheat Thins.

**Nations are just like individuals. Loan them money and you lose their friendship.**

—*Will Rogers*

Ω

## PARTY ORANGE BALLS

1 (12-ounce) box vanilla wafers, crushed
3 cups sugar
1 (6-ounce) can frozen orange juice
½ cup butter, melted
½ cup chopped pecans
½ cup flake coconut

Mix all ingredients except coconut. Shape into small balls and roll in coconut. Freeze and serve frozen. Makes 3 dozen.

## FRIED CHEESE BALLS

½ cup grated cheese
½ cup bread crumbs
Salt
Pepper
2 egg whites, beaten
½ teaspoon baking powder

Mix cheese, bread crumbs and seasonings. Fold in the beaten egg whites and baking powder. Shape into tiny balls and fry at 390° in deep oil. Serve with a dip.

Ω

## FRUIT AND CHEESE KABOBS

**That's all there is to success is satisfaction.**

*—Will Rogers*

1 cup plain yogurt
2 tablespoons honey
1 cup grapes
1 cup (¾-inch) pineapple cubes
1 cup strawberries
1 cup (1-inch) banana pieces
1 cup (¾-inch) cheddar cheese cubes
1 cup (¾-inch) Swiss cheese cubes
8 (8-inch) skewers
Lemon juice

In small bowl, stir together yogurt and honey. Cover and refrigerate at least 30 minutes. Dip fruit pieces in lemon juice to prevent discoloration. Assemble kabobs by alternating fruit pieces and cheese cubes on skewers. Serve with dip.

## HONEY-MUSTARD DIP

**Will Rogers Memorial Carolyn Diffenbaugh**

*2 cups salad dressing or mayonnaise*
*2 tablespoons yellow mustard*
*1 tablespoon Dijon mustard*
*1 tablespoon cider vinegar*
*½ cup honey*
*Dash red pepper*

Combine all ingredients in a bowl and mix well. Great with vegetables, salads and sandwiches. Makes 1 quart.

Ω

## NUTTY CREAM CHEESE SPREAD

*1 (8-ounce) package cream cheese, softened*
*2 tablespoons soft butter*
*2 tablespoons milk*
*3 tablespoons crushed pecans*
*½ teaspoon salt*
*1 cup flour*

Let butter and cheese come to room temperature and mix thoroughly. Add remaining ingredients and blend well. Shape into 2 or 3 rolls. Wrap in wax paper and chill. Heat oven to 375°. Slice rolls ¼ inch thick. Bake on ungreased baking sheet 10 to12 minutes or until slightly browned on edges. Makes 6-8 dozen.

When you are worried you know what you are worried about, but when you are "confused" it's when you don't know enough about a thing to be worried.

—*Will Rogers*

**[37]**

## GARBAGE SNACKS

*2 sticks margarine, melted*
*2 tablespoons Worcestershire sauce*
*Dash Tabasco*
*1 teaspoon garlic salt*
*1 teaspoon celery salt*
*1 teaspoon onion salt*
*1 pound peanuts*
*1 box pretzel sticks*
*4 cups Cheerios*
*4 cups Rice Chex*
*4 cups Wheat Chex*

Mix margarine, Worcestershire sauce, Tabasco, garlic, celery salt and onion salt in a large pan. One at a time add remaining ingredients, stirring thoroughly to coat. Cook at 200° for 6 hours. Stir mixture occasionally. Store in tight container.

∩

## OLIVE SURPRISE

*¼ cup butter, softened*
*1 cup grated, sharp cheddar cheese*
*½ cup flour*
*3 dozen stuffed green olives*

Cream butter and cheese until blended, add flour and mix well. Chill dough 20 minutes. Drain olives and dry. Shape small portion of dough around each olive. Place olives on cookie sheet and bake at 375° for 15 minutes. Serve hot or cold.

## OKIE NUTS

¼ cup butter
2 cups walnuts
1 tablespoon sugar
¼ teaspoon allspice
½ teaspoon cinnamon

Melt butter in saucepan and add nuts. Stir gently over low heat for 2 minutes. Sprinkle nuts with sugar and spices until well coated. Cool on cookie sheet.

∩

## SUGARED PECANS

1 pound pecans
2 tablespoons butter
1 teaspoon cinnamon
½ cup sugar

Put pecans in saucepan and add butter and cinnamon. Melt butter and stir until nuts are coated. Pour on cookie sheet and sprinkle with sugar.

∩

## SHIPTER DELIGHT

1 (8-ounce) package cream cheese, softened
¾ cup packed brown sugar
1 tablespoon vanilla
6 apples, cut into wedges
Chopped peanuts

In a small bowl, beat cream cheese, brown sugar and vanilla until smooth. Spread mixture on apples and top with nuts. Makes 6 servings.

A flock of Democrats will replace a mess of Republicans. It won't mean a thing. They will go in like all the rest of 'em. Go in on promises and come out on alibis.

—Will Rogers

## SIDEWINDERS

*2 medium potatoes, cut into 8 wedges*
*Vegetable oil*
*Seasoned salt*
*¾ cup sour cream*
*½ cup shredded cheddar cheese*

Place potato wedges on baking sheet. Brush with oil and sprinkle with seasoned salt. Broil until brown, approximately 5 minutes. Turn, brush with oil and sprinkle with seasoned salt. Broil until tender. Spoon sour cream onto the center of a large serving platter and sprinkle with cheese. Arrange potato wedges around sour cream.

∩

## INDIVIDUAL PIZZAS

*3 English muffins, split, toasted*
*6 tablespoons pizza sauce*
*18 thin slices pepperoni*
*¼ cup sliced mushrooms*
*¾ cup shredded mozzarella cheese*

Spread each English muffin half with 1 tablespoon of pizza sauce. Top each muffin with 3 slices of pepperoni, a few of the mushroom slices and 1 tablespoon of the mozzarella cheese. Place on cookie sheet or pizza pan. Bake at 375° until cheese melts. Makes 6 individual pizzas.

## PIZZA CRACKERS

4 saltine crackers
3 teaspoons pizza sauce
1 slice mozzarella cheese, quartered
4 slices pepperoni

Spread one side of each cracker with pizza sauce. Top each with a piece of cheese and a slice of pepperoni. Arrange crackers on a paper-towel-lined plate. Microwave at 50% (medium) for 30 seconds or until cheese melts. Makes 1 serving.

Ω

## SAUSAGE-APPLE APPETIZER

4 packages smokie links, cut in one-inch pieces
1 cup packed brown sugar
3 medium onions, sliced
4 large apples, peeled and sliced

Put links in casserole or baking dish. Cover with brown sugar, onions, and apples. Bake covered at 250° for 1 hour. Makes 20-25 servings.

During our World's Richest Roping and Western Art Show at our Bushyhead Ranch, we would usually have 15-20 friends stay with us. Of course, beef was the main fare, but this was a great appetizer. It's been used for a few political gatherin's too! (Donna McSpadden)

Saw in the paper where down in Peru five people were killed after a football game. Up here we don't kill our football players. We just make coaches out of the smartest ones and send the other to the state legislature.

—Will Rogers

[41]

## WACKY POPCORN

*1 big bowl popped popcorn*
*1/ pound butter*
*2 cloves garlic*
*1 tablespoon chopped parsley*
*1 tablespoon chopped green onions*
*Salt*

Melt butter in skillet and put in garlic in large pieces so you can see them to lift them out. When butter is delicately brown, remove garlic, add parsley and green onions and pour over the popcorn, salt to taste. Do this the day before you serve it.

**On prohibition: Most people vote dry and drink wet.**

*—Will Rogers*

Ω

## CANTELOUPE PUNCH

*1 cantaloupe, peeled, cut up*
*10 maraschino cherries*
*1 tablespoon lemon juice*
*1 (46-ounce) can pineapple juice, chilled*
*2 (7-ounce) chilled bottles ginger ale*
*Ice*

Put cantaloupe, cherries and lemon juice in blender. Add pineapple juice to cover and blend until puréed. Combine with remaining juice in punch bowl. Add ginger ale. Serve over ice. Makes 2¾ quarts.

## BOOMER'S PARADISE PUNCH

*2 cups orange juice*
*1 cup lemon juice*
*4 cups apple cider*
*1 cup sugar*

Combine all ingredients and stir until sugar is dissolved. Pour over ice cubes and garnish with mint leaves.

Ω

## ANYTIME PUNCH

*2 cups sugar*
*1 ½ cups water*
*1 cup lemon juice*
*1 cup orange juice*
*1 (6-ounce) can frozen pineapple juice concentrate, thawed*
*2 quarts ginger ale, chilled*

In a saucepan, bring sugar and water to a boil. Boil for 10 minutes and remove from heat. Stir in lemon, orange and pineapple juices. Refrigerate. Just before serving, combine with ginger ale in large punch bowl. Makes 16-20 servings.

Ω

## 1920'S RHUBARB PUNCH

*1 quart diced rhubarb*
*1 quart water*
*1 grated orange rind*
*1 cup sugar*

Simmer rhubarb in water until very tender. Strain and add orange rind and sugar and stir until sugar is dissolved. Cool and chill on ice before serving.

> Hunt out and talk about the good that is in the other fellow's church, not the bad, and you will do away with all this religious hatred you hear so much about nowadays.
>
> —*Will Rogers*

## SUNNY SUNDAY PUNCH

*1 (3-ounce) package orange-pineapple flavored
    gelatin*
*1 cup boiling water*
*1 (6-ounce) can frozen orange juice, thawed*
*1 (6-ounce) can frozen pineapple juice
    concentrate, thawed*
*5 cups cold water, divided*
*1 (28-ounce) bottle ginger ale, chilled*
*Ice cubes*
*Orange slices*

Put gelatin in 1 cup boiling water and mix until gelatin is dissolved. Add pineapple juice, orange juice and 1 cup cold water to gelatin mixture and blend until well mixed. Pour mixture into punch bowl and stir in remaining 4 cups cold water. Add ice cubes and pour in chilled ginger ale. Float orange slices. Makes 2¾ quarts.

**Give America a one-piece bathing suit, a hamburger, and five gallons of gasoline, and they are just as tickled as a movie star with a new divorce.**
*—Will Rogers*

∩

## PEACHY-CREAM MILK SHAKE

*1 cup milk, divided*
*1 cup sliced peaches*
*1 pint peach ice cream*
*Sugar*
*Peach slices*

Put ¼ cup milk and sliced peaches in blender and blend until smooth. Spoon in ice cream and blend until softened. Add ¾ cup milk and blend well. Sweeten with sugar, if desired. Pour in tall glasses. Garnish each serving with fresh peach slices. Makes 4 servings.

# TORNADO SHAKE

*2½ cups cold milk, divided*
*4 teaspoons instant coffee powder*
*½ cup chocolate syrup*
*1 quart chocolate ice cream*

Put 1 cup milk, coffee powder and chocolate syrup in blender container with ice cream. Blend until smooth. Add rest of milk and blend. Makes 6 servings.

∩

# STRAWBERRY-BANANA SHAKE

*1 cup cold milk*
*1 banana*
*1 pint strawberry ice cream*

Blend together until smooth. Makes 2 to 3 servings.

∩

# MALTED MILK SHAKE

*1 cup cold milk*
*¼ cup chocolate syrup*
*2 tablespoons malted milk powder*
*1 pint vanilla ice cream*

Put cold milk, chocolate syrup and malted milk powder in blender with ice cream. Blend until mixture is smooth. Makes 3 servings.

Preachers say, 'Let no man put asunder.' And a quarter of the married world is asunder in less than six months.

—*Will Rogers*

**[45]**

## OH GOODIE EGGNOG

*4 egg yolks, beaten*
*8 tablespoons sugar*
*½ teaspoon salt*
*2 teaspoons vanilla*
*2 quarts milk*
*4 egg whites*
*Nutmeg*

Beat egg yolks until thick. Add sugar, salt, vanilla and milk. Beat until thoroughly blended. Beat egg whites separately, then fold into mixture. Pour into tall glasses or eggnog cups and sprinkle with nutmeg.

Ω

## GULLY WASHER COFFEE

*½ cup instant cocoa mix*
*¼ cup instant coffee crystals*
*4 cups hot water*

Combine cocoa mix, coffee crystals and hot water. Stir until blended. Makes 4 servings.

Ω

## 1920'S FRONT PORCH LEMONADE

*1 ¼ cup sugar*
*½ cup boiling water*
*1 ½ cups fresh lemon juice*
*4 ½ cups cold water*
*Lemon slices*

Combine sugar and boiling water, stirring until sugar dissolves. Add lemon juice and cold water and mix well. Chill and serve over ice. Garnish with lemon slices.

## SUNSET SLUSH

1 (12-ounce) can peach nectar
1 (6-ounce) can frozen orange juice, thawed
1 tablespoon lemon juice
1 cup crushed ice

Put all ingredients in blender and blend well. Makes 3 to 4 servings.

Ω

## CHOCOLATE-BANANA SPLENDER

1 banana
2 cups cold chocolate-flavored milk
¼ teaspoon vanilla

Peel banana and cut into 1-inch pieces. Wrap banana in foil and freeze solid. Place chocolate milk, frozen pieces of banana and vanilla in blender. Blend until banana is puréed and ingredients are combined. Makes 3 servings.

Ω

## BUCKSHOT BLUSH

2 cups cold buttermilk
2 nectarines, chilled, peeled, cut in pieces
¼ cup packed brown sugar

Combine all ingredients and blend until nectarines are puréed. Serve mixture in chilled glasses. Makes 4 servings.

I've got some advice on the stock market. Take your money, buy good stock, hold it till it goes up, then sell it. If it don't go up, don't buy it.

—Will Rogers

## ORANGE COOLER

*1 (6-ounce) can frozen orange juice, thawed*
*1 cup milk*
*1 cup water*
*½ cup sugar*
*1½ teaspoons vanilla*
*12 ice cubes*

Place ingredients in blender and blend until well mixed. Makes 3 servings.

∩

## STRAWBERRY FROSTY DELIGHT

*1 (3-ounce) package strawberry flavored gelatin*
*1 cup boiling water*
*1 quart cold milk, divided*
*1 quart strawberry ice cream, divided*

Put strawberry flavored gelatin and boiling water in blender and blend at low speed until gelatin is dissolved. Pour ½ cup gelatin mixture into measuring cup and set aside. Add ½ the milk to remaining mixture in blender and blend on low speed. Add half the strawberry ice cream and blend until smooth. Pour into tall glasses and repeat with reserved gelatin, milk and ice cream. Makes 6 servings. *(Mary McFall)*

**There ought to be a law against anybody going to Europe till they had seen the things in this country.**

—*Will Rogers*

# SIDEKICKS

[soups, salads and vegetables]

Step by step Will Rogers climbed the ladder of success, and through his kindliness, his abiding love and faith in God and humanity, through his clear vision and deep understanding, he achieved a personality that will live on and on. His ability in grasping a situation and seeing through it clearly and rapidly was all but uncanny.

**Betty and Will Rogers**

I have been asked, "Where did Will get his wit?" Primarily from our mother, but the inheritance might never have come into fruition had he been less of a student. He studied. To the majority of his vast audience they thought his wit was a divine gift. They made no allowance for the hours he put in reading, reading, reading. How else could he have quoted our great authors as he did? His frequent references to Shakespeare and his matchless plays and his quotations from the Bible were given most accurately.

As a brother he was loving, generous and considerate. As a husband and father he was unsurpassed in thoughtfulness and deep appreciation of wife and children.

**A mixed-blood Cherokee cowboy, actor, comedian, radio personality, speaker, and humorist taken into the hearts of the American people as no other private citizen before or since.**

*—Jim Rogers, Will Roger's son*

To those who stood in need of cheer he brought smiles and happiness. He lightened the loads of those who were bearing heavy crosses. He brought courage to the disheartened. We will ever cherish his memory and good deeds.

*—Sallie Rogers McSpadden,*
*Will Rogers' sister*

Will Rogers loved the outdoors, and it is reflected in the living room at the Santa Monica Ranch. The high ceilings would accommodate Will's rope tricks.

Will and Betty Rogers were out riding one evening when it was suggested that they go to a moving picture theater. Will had not

"Mom, I've been listening to that joke for five years." "Hush, son, I've had to listen to it for fifteen."

A polo playing family. They were all excellent horsemen. Jimmie, Mary, Will, Jr., and Will. The polo grounds Will built at his ranch in Santa Monica is still used today.

seen his last picture, so they drove to a theater where it was showing, parked the automobile, and entered the lobby. Then Will found he had no money in his pockets. "Let's go home," he said. It never occurred to him that he could enter any theater in the United States with no more credentials than his well known face.

The Rogers family, 1916-17, Long Island, New York. Will was working in the Zeigfeld Follies. Will and Jimmie in front, Mary, "Bill", and Betty in back.

Betty Blake did not think show business was a very stable profession. She agreed to marry Will Rogers only on the condition that once he completed the tour he had booked at $200 per week, he would return to Oklahoma and settle down. But at the end of that tour he was offered $300 a week. Betty agreed that he

Betty and Will Rogers with their children, Will, Jr., Mary, and Jimmie.

I can see the same boy—grown older, but not grown up; though a little gray and a little stout. And it's not Comanche he's on—it's old Soapsuds. But he still has a rope on his saddle and he still wants to go somewhere.

—*Betty Rogers*

A barbecue at the Will Rogers Ranch in Santa Monica, California. Will's oldest sister, Sallie McSpadden, Will Rogers, Sallie's husband, Tom, and Betty Rogers (seated).

should take the booking. Their return to Claremore kept getting postponed. Betty never made him keep his promise—but was a steady helpmate as he became the highest paid entertainer in the world.

Will never said a mean thing, he refused to gossip, and would have nothing to do with such talk. When an absent person was

was being raked over the coals by a group, Will invariably found something to say in his favor. Will wouldn't pick on anyone who was down, and he always resisted when others were doing so.

—*Betty Rogers*

Will Rogers loved brown Mexican beans. One day he told Betty, "Betty, I want those Mexican beans every night." The first night Betty prepared a small dish of the beans, and Will said, "That's not what I want. I love them and want a lot of those beans." The next day Betty served a large four quart bowl of these favorite beans—and did so each night for the next month. By that time Will was sick and tired of Mexican beans and had to call it quits.

—*Told by Hal Roach, Director*

**Clem McSpadden, great nephew of Will Rogers was raised on the Dog Iron Ranch, birthplace of Will Rogers. His father was ranch manager for Will. Clem became a well known figure in Oklahoma politics, twice President Pro Tempore of the Oklahoma State Senate where he served eighteen years. He was also elected United States Congressman from Oklahoma's Second District. He is best known nationally as a professional rodeo announcer.**

**Will Rogers in polo attire in front of dressing rooms on the Fox Studios lot.**

## FRENCH ONION SOUP

*2 pounds sweet onions, sliced*
*½ stick butter*
*1 tablespoon flour*
*¼ teaspoon salt*
*2 (13¾-ounce) cans beef broth*
*¼ cup dry sherry*
*1 cup water*
*1 (4¾-inch) loaf Italian bread*
*½ pound Fontina cheese, shredded*

**Good character is like good soup—it's usually homemade.**

—*Will Rogers*

In Dutch oven over high heat, cook onions in butter 15 minutes or until tender, stirring often. Stir in flour and salt until blended. Add beef broth, sherry and water and heat to boiling. Reduce heat to low, cover and simmer 20 minutes. Slice bread and toast in oven at 450°. Put onion mixture in 4 oven-safe bowls. Place bread on top and top with shredded cheese. Bake soup at 450° for 20 minutes or until cheese is melted and top is brown. (Cindy Baugham)

## HANGOVER CHEESE SOUP

*¼ cup butter or margarine*
*½ cup all-purpose flour*
*2 tablespoons instant onion flakes*
*1 (12-ounce) can evaporated milk*
*1 cup milk, divided*
*1 (16-ounce) jar processed cheese spread*
*1 (12-ounce) can beer*

In a saucepan, melt butter and blend in the flour and onion flakes. Add the evaporated milk and milk, ⅓ at a time, blending after each addition. Keep stirring until mixture thickens and bubbles. Stir in cheese until melted and smooth. Blend in beer and cook 5 minutes more. Makes 6 servings.

## LIGHTNING POTATO SOUP

*1 pound ground beef*
*4 cups diced, peeled potatoes*
*1 small onion, diced*
*3 (8-ounce) cans tomato sauce*
*4 cups water*
*2 teaspoons salt*
*1½ teaspoons pepper*
*1 teaspoon hot pepper sauce*

In a large kettle, brown ground beef and drain. Add potatoes, onions and tomato sauce and mix well. Stir in water, salt, pepper and hot sauce and bring to a boil. Reduce heat and simmer for 1 hour or until potatoes are tender and soup has thickened. Makes 6 to 8 servings.

## PAT'S POTATO SOUP

*3 potatoes, diced*
*½ cup diced celery*
*½ cup diced onion*
*1 large carrot, diced*
*1 teaspoon parsley flakes*
*½ teaspoon salt*
*2 chicken bouillon cubes*
*1½ cups water*
*2 cups milk*
*2 teaspoons flour*
*½ pound Velveeta cheese, cubed*

**A mother and a dog are the only two things that possess eternal love. No matter how you treat 'em you still have their love and understandin'.**
—*Will Rogers*

In large saucepan, put potatoes, celery, onion, carrot, parsley flakes, chicken bouillon cubes and water. Cook until tender and add more water, if needed. Add milk and flour to saucepan and mix well. Add cheese and stir often so cheese will not burn. cook on low heat. (Pat Howell)

**[57]**

## CHEESE POTATO SOUP

*6 potatoes, cubed*
*1 large onion, chopped*
*½ cup shredded carrots*
*½ cup shredded green pepper*
*Water*
*1 cup Velveeta cheese, cubed*
*1 cup milk*
*1 cup sour cream*
*½ stick margarine*

Cook potatoes, onions, carrots and green pepper in boiling water until tender. Pour off enough water just enough to cover vegetables. Add cheese and melt, stirring constantly. Add milk and sour cream, stirring constantly, and heat just to boiling. Remove from heat and serve. (Cindy Baughman)

∩

## CINDY'S BROCCOLI CHEESE SOUP

*6 tablespoons butter*
*1 cup finely chopped carrots*
*1 cup finely chopped onions*
*½ cup finely chopped celery*
*2 cups chopped broccoli*
*½ cup flour*
*2 cups chicken broth*
*½ tablespoon salt*
*4 cups milk*
*3 cups shredded cheese*

Melt butter and cook veggies until tender. Add flour, broth and salt. Heat until thick and bubbly. Add milk and cheese, stirring constantly. When well blended serve. (Cindy Baugham)

**Mother's Day was thought up by some fellow with a hurting conscience. He said, "Let's give Mother a day and in return she'll give us the other 364.**

—*Will Rogers*

## SOUTH FORTY BARLEY SOUP

*2 cups cooked, cubed beef*
*3 cups water*
*1 cup frozen, cut green beans*
*1 cup sliced carrots*
*¼ cup quick-cooking barley*
*1 tablespoon instant beef bouillon granules*
*1 tablespoon dried thyme leaves*

In large saucepan, combine all ingredients. Bring to boil and reduce heat to low. Cover tightly and simmer until barley is tender. Makes 4 servings.

∩

## SODBUSTER PEA SOUP

*1 cup dried split peas*
*2 quarts water*
*1 tablespoon flour*
*2 tablespoons butter*
*½ tablespoon celery salt*
*1 teaspoon onion juice*
*Salt*
*Pepper*

Soak peas overnight. Cook with water, bring to a boil and simmer until soft. Rub through a sieve. Heat and thicken with flour and butter. Add celery salt and onion juice and stir until smooth. Season to taste with salt and pepper. (Mary McFall)

Live your life so that when you lose it, you are ahead. Live your life so that you wouldn't be afraid to sell the family parrot to the town gossip.

—*Will Rogers*

## MIDWEST CORN CHOWDER

*2 slices salt pork, diced*
*1 large onion, sliced*
*3 potatoes, cubed*
*1 pint boiling water*
*1 (15-ounce) can kernel corn, drained*
*1 quart milk*
*½ teaspoon salt*
*¼ teaspoon pepper*

Fry pork until crisp. Add onion and cook gently until yellow. Add potatoes and water. Cover and cook slowly until potatoes are tender. Add corn, milk and seasonings. Bring to scalding point, stirring constantly. Serve at once.

∩

## ROUGHNECK BEAN SOUP

*3 slices bacon*
*2 cups dried beans*
*4 cups water*
*1 tablespoon flour*
*1 tablespoon butter, melted*
*Salt*
*Pepper*

Cook bacon and add to beans. Add cold water and cook until beans are soft. Add more water, if needed so soup will not be too thick. Mix flour and butter and put into soup. Cook 15 minutes. Salt and pepper to taste.

## CREAMY BROCCOLI SOUP

1 (10-ounce) package chopped broccoli
2 cups milk
2 tablespoons butter
1 cup instant potato flakes
2 teaspoons minced onions
1 cup chicken broth
½ teaspoon salt

Cook broccoli according to package directions and put undrained broccoli in blender. In same saucepan heat milk and butter (do not boil). Stir in potato flakes and onions. Add milk mixture to broccoli and blend well, stirring constantly. Return mixture to saucepan and add broth. Salt to taste. Simmer 10 minutes on low heat. For thinner soup, add more milk. Makes 6 (½-cup) servings.

∩

## CREAM OF ASPARAGUS SOUP

¾ cup water
¾ teaspoon salt
1 pound fresh asparagus, chopped
1 cup light cream
2 tablespoons butter or margarine

Heat water and salt to boiling. Add asparagus, cover and simmer until asparagus is tender. Add cream to mixture and blend until smooth and asparagus is very tender. Add butter and heat thoroughly. Dot each serving with butter. Makes 4 servings.

**My wife has been tryin' for twenty-some years to raise to maturity four children— three by birth and one by marriage.**

*—Will Rogers*

## OYSTER STEW

*4 tablespoons butter, divided*
*1 pint oysters, undrained*
*2 cups milk*
*1 can cream*
*Salt*
*Pepper*
*Dash Worcestershire*

In saucepan, melt 2 tablespoons butter and add oysters, undrained. Simmer until oysters curl. Add milk, cream, salt, pepper and Worcester-shire sauce. Heat to hot, stirring constantly.

∩

## SHRIMP BISQUE SOUP

*2½ cups milk*
*2 tablespoons butter*
*1 tablespoon flour*
*1 (4½-ounce) can shrimp, drained*
*¼ teaspoon dried mustard*
*Salt*
*Pepper*

Put all ingredients in saucepan and stir until well mixed. Cook, stirring occasionally, until thick and bubbly. Makes 4 servings.

**The two finest things that can happen to a man is to have a good wife and to know that he's accepted by the people he comes from.**

—*Will Rogers*

## CREAM OF MUSHROOM SOUP

*2 tablespoons butter*
*½ cup chopped onions*
*¼ pound mushrooms, sliced*
*2 tablespoons flour*
*½ teaspoon salt*
*¼ teaspoon pepper*
*Milk*

Melt butter and cook onion until soft, but not brown. Remove onion and add sliced caps and stems of mushrooms and cook gently for 5 minutes. Add flour and seasonings; stir well and add milk. Stir constantly and cook until smooth and thick.

∩

## 1920s CHICKEN SOUP

*1 cup chopped chicken*
*1 quart chicken broth*
*1 quart water*
*1 cup rice*
*1 rib celery, chopped*
*1 onion, chopped*
*Salt*
*Pepper*

Mix all ingredients, cover and cook about 1 hour or until everything is tender.

**You know, women always could endure more than men, not only physically, but mentally. Did you ever get a peek at some of the husbands?**

—*Will Rogers*

## CRUNCHY CHICKEN SALAD

¾ cup salad dressing
1 tablespoon sugar
1 teaspoon grated lemon peel
1 tablespoon lemon juice
½ teaspoon ground ginger
¼ teaspoon salt
2 cups cut-up, cooked chicken
1 cup seedless grapes, red or green
2 ribs celery, chopped
½ cup almond slivers

Mix salad dressing, sugar, lemon peel, lemon juice, ginger and salt. Stir in chicken, grapes and celery. Cook almonds with 1 tablespoon sugar over low heat, stirring constantly until sugar is melted and almonds are coated; let cool. Spoon crunchy salad into lettuce-lined bowl. Sprinkle with almonds.

Ω

## HAM-PINEAPPLE SALAD

1½ cups cooked, cubed ham
2 ounces Swiss cheese, cubed
1 cup seedless grapes, halved
1 (8-ounce) can crushed pineapple, divided
1 cup cream-style cottage cheese
2 tablespoons lemon juice
4 cups torn lettuce

In large bowl, combine ham, cheese and grapes, toss lightly and chill. Drain pineapple, reserving ¼ cup syrup. Blend cottage cheese, crushed pineapple, reserved pineapple syrup and lemon juice until smooth. Pour desired amount of dressing over salad and toss to mix. Serve on lettuce. Makes 4 servings.

## OVERNIGHT PASTA SALAD

*2 cooked, boneless chicken breasts, chopped*
*1 package cooked shell macaroni*
*1 cucumber, peeled and chopped*
*1 rib celery, diced*
*1 (8-ounce) jar salad dressing*
*1 (8-ounce) container sour cream*
*Salt*
*Pepper*

Cool chicken and macaroni and mix together. Add cucumber, celery, salad dressing and sour cream to macaroni and mix well. Season with salt and pepper. Refrigerate overnight before serving.

Ω

## TERRIFIC TURKEY-TACO SALAD

*1 pound ground turkey breast*
*½ cup taco sauce*
*6 cups torn lettuce*
*1 cup corn chips*
*½ cup drained, pitted, ripe olives*
*2 tomatoes, chopped*
*1 small bell pepper, chopped*
*1 cup shredded cheddar cheese*
*1 tablespoon oil*

Put oil in 10-inch skillet and cook turkey over medium heat until no longer pink. Drain and stir in taco sauce and heat until hot. Toss lettuce, corn chips, olives, tomatoes and bell pepper in large bowl. Spoon hot turkey mixture over lettuce mixture. Toss and sprinkle with cheese.

> **It's all right to fix the world, but you better get your own smokehouse full of meat first.**
>
> —*Will Rogers*

## OUT-OF-THE-PAST CHICKEN SALAD

*2 cups cooked, cubed chicken*
*1 cup diced celery*
*1 tablespoon lemon juice*
*1 cup sweet green grapes, halved*
*1 tablespoon sugar*
*Salt*
*Pepper*
*¼ cup almonds*
*Mayonnaise*
*Lettuce*

Toss together chicken, celery, lemon juice and grapes. Add remaining ingredients and mix in mayonnaise to coat. Chill thoroughly. Arrange on lettuce.

Ω

## CHICKEN–MACARONI SALAD

*2 cups cooked, cooled macaroni*
*1 cup diced cucumber*
*1 ½ cups cooked, cubed chicken*
*1 tablespoon grated onion*
*¾ cup mayonnaise*
*½ teaspoon salt*
*¼ teaspoon pepper*
*Lettuce*

Combine all ingredients except lettuce and toss together until blended. Chill. Serve on lettuce. Makes 4 to 6 servings.

## CANTALOUPE CHICKEN SALAD

*1 cup whipping cream*
*½ cup sour cream*
*2 tablespoons chopped, fresh tarragon leaves*
*1 teaspoon grated lime peel*
*2 tablespoons chopped fresh dill*
*¼ teaspoon salt*
*6 cups cooked chicken, cubed*
*3 cups cut-up cantaloupe*
*½ cup toasted, slivered almonds*
*1 cucumber, peeled, sliced, halved*

In chilled small mixer bowl, beat chilled whipping cream at high speed until stiff peaks form. Gently stir in sour cream. Add tarragon leaves, lime peel, fresh dill and salt. In large bowl, combine remaining ingredients. Add cream mixture and toss to coat. Cover and refrigerate at least 2 hours. Makes 8 servings.

Ω

## OUT TO SEA SALAD

*1 cup cooked, chopped shrimp*
*1 cup diced celery*
*1 cup lettuce hearts, chopped*
*1 teaspoon lemon juice*
*1 teaspoon finely minced onion*
*Salt*
*Salad dressing*
*1 teaspoon sugar*
*Lettuce*
*Tomatoes*

Combine shrimp, celery and lettuce pieces. Mix lemon juice, onion and salt and pour over shrimp. Mix salad dressing and sugar and add to shrimp mixture. Serve on crisp lettuce. Garnish with tomato sections. Makes 4 servings.

**When you have to be told what to say when you meet anyone, you are not the one to meet them.**

*—Will Rogers*

## 1932 SALMON SALAD

*4 cups boiled, diced potatoes*
*1 (15-ounce) can salmon*
*1 cup chopped pickles*
*2 hard-boiled eggs, diced*
*1 egg, beaten*
*1 cup cream*
*1 cup vinegar*
*2 teaspoons sugar*
*Salt*
*Pepper*

Mix together, potatoes, salmon, pickles and hard-boiled eggs. In saucepan, put egg, cream, vinegar, sugar, salt and pepper. Bring to a boil, cool and pour over salmon mixture. (Mrs. B. Aosburn)

∩

## TUNA SALAD DELIGHT

*1 (6-ounce) can tuna, drained*
*1 cup chopped celery*
*1 cup finely shredded cabbage*
*¾ cup salad dressing*
*½ teaspoon sugar*

Mix tuna and vegetables. Combine salad dressing and sugar and add to tuna mixture. Place on lettuce leaves. Makes 6 servings.

## DELICIOUS LUNCH SALAD

¼ cup butter or margarine
¼ teaspoon garlic salt
1 quart (½-inch) soft bread cubes
1 (10-ounce) package frozen peas
1 (4½-ounce) can cooked shrimp
¼ cup salad dressing
1 teaspoon sugar
½ teaspoon salt
1 green onion, chopped
¼ cup canned mushrooms, drained
1 tablespoon lemon juice

Melt butter in a large skillet, blend in garlic and add soft bread cubes. Stir over low heat until brown on all sides, turning them often. Set aside and allow them to cool. Cook peas in small amount of water, drain and cool. Clean shrimp. Combine remaining ingredients and refrigerate. At serving time, stir in toasted bread and serve each portion on a bed of lettuce. Makes 4 to 6 servings.

**My ancestors didn't come over on the Mayflower, but they met the boat.**

—Will Rogers

Ω

## BRUNCH OR LUNCH SALAD

1 apple, unpeeled, chopped
3 carrots, chopped
3 oranges, peeled, diced
½ cup raisins
¾ cup salad dressing
1 tablespoon sugar
Lettuce

In large bowl, combine all ingredients except lettuce and toss lightly. Chill before serving. Serve on lettuce cups.

## DELIGHTFUL IN-SEASON SALAD

¼ cup orange juice

2 tablespoons oil

1 tablespoon red wine vinegar

1 tablespoon honey

1 teaspoon ground ginger

4 cups torn romaine lettuce

3 peeled oranges, chopped

2 peeled kiwi fruit, sliced

1 cup strawberries, sliced

In small bowl stir together, orange juice, oil, red wine vinegar, honey and ground ginger and mix well. In large bowl, place torn lettuce. Pour 2 tablespoons dressing over lettuce and toss to coat. On individual salad plates, place lettuce and arrange oranges, kiwi and strawberries on top. Drizzle with remaining dressing. Makes 8 servings.

Ω

## AUTUMN SALAD

1 (15-ounce) can crushed pineapple with juice

⅔ cup sugar

1 box lime flavored gelatin

1 (8-ounce) package cream cheese

1 cup chopped apples

1 cup chopped celery

1 cup pecan pieces

1 carton whipped topping

**How they can call it traffic when it ceases to move, I don't understand.**

—*Will Rogers*

Boil pineapple and sugar for 2 minutes. Add dry gelatin and mix well. Add cream cheese; dissolve well and let cool. Add apples, celery, pecans and whipped topping. Chill and serve. (Loistine Norfleet)

## LINDA LEE'S BEAN SALAD

1 (8-ounce) can red kidney beans, drained
2 hard-boiled eggs, chopped
2½ tablespoons chopped onions
1 tablespoon relish
1 tablespoon sugar
½ cup salad dressing
Dash mustard

In bowl, mix together the beans, eggs, onions and relish. Combine sugar, salad dressing and mustard and mix with other ingredients. Chill 1 hour.

∩

## ATTRACTIVE ASPARAGUS SALAD

Green pepper, topped, seeded
24 ribs cooked asparagus, chilled
Lettuce leaves
French dressing
½ tablespoon tomato catsup

Cut green pepper into 6 rings about ⅓-inch wide. Slip 4 ribs of cold asparagus through each ring and arrange each serving on crisp lettuce on individual salad plates or on a platter. Serve with French dressing mixed with catsup. Makes 6 servings.

I've got a solution to the traffic problem. That is that no car be allowed on the road until it's paid for.

—Will Rogers

[71]

## OVERNIGHT GREEN BEAN SALAD

*2 cups green beans*
*3 tablespoons French dressing*
*2 tablespoons chopped onions*
*3 tablespoons grated*
*cheddar cheese*
*1 red onion, sliced*

Marinate beans in dressing and onion overnight. Add cheese and garnish with red onion rings. Makes 4 servings. (Mary McFall)

**More people should work for their dinner instead of dressin' for it.**

—*Will Rogers*

## HOT SPINACH SALAD

*¼ cup vinegar*
*½ cup water*
*2 green onions, chopped*
*1 teaspoon salt*
*1 quart spinach*
*1 hard-boiled egg, chopped*
*4 slices cooked bacon, crumbled*

Combine vinegar and water and heat. Add onion and salt and pour hot mixture over spinach. Toss until wilted. Sprinkle egg and bacon over top. Makes 6 servings.

## CHERRY PEPPER SALAD

*½ cup vinegar*
*2 cups packed brown sugar*
*1 to 2 cans sauerkraut,*
   *finely chopped*
*1 cup finely chopped celery*
*1 cup finely chopped green pepper*
*1 cup finely chopped onion*
*½ cup finely chopped pimento*
*½ cup finely chopped cherry peppers*

Bring vinegar and brown sugar to a boil and let cool. Combine all ingredients and pour dressing over top and toss. Let cool and serve. (This recipe has been in the family since 1960 and served on every holiday.)

∩

## BROCCOLI SALAD TOSS

*1 bunch broccoli*
*1 pound bacon*
*½ cup raisins*
*1 cup sunflower seeds*
*½ red onion, thinly sliced*

Cut broccoli into small flowerets. Cook bacon until crisp and crumble. Add raisins, sunflower seeds and onions.

**Broccoli Sauce:**

*2 cups mayonnaise*
*¼ cup milk*
*⅓ cup sugar*
*2 tablespoons vinegar*

Mix together all ingredients. Pour over salad about 1 or 2 hours before serving and chill. Makes 8 servings.

**They ought to pass a constitutional amendment prohibiting anybody from learning anything. If it works as good as the one on prohibition did, in five years we would have the smartest race of people on earth.**
—*Will Rogers*

## VEGGIE CRUNCH SALAD

*4 cups fresh cauliflowerets*
*4 cups fresh broccoli florets*
*1 red onion, chopped*
*2 cups cherry tomatoes, halved*
*1 tablespoon vinegar*
*1 cup salad dressing*
*½ cup sour cream*
*2 tablespoons sugar*

In large salad bowl, combine all vegetables. Mix remaining ingredients separately until smooth, pour dressing over vegetables and toss to coat. Cover and chill for 2 hours.

∩

## OLD-TIME POTATO SALAD

**Nobody can fall out and get as sore at each other as kinfolks.**

—*Will Rogers*

*3 cups diced, cooked potatoes*
*4 hard-cooked eggs, diced*
*1 cup diced celery*
*2 tablespoons chopped onions*
*2 tablespoons chopped green peppers*
*2 tablespoons chopped sweet pickles*
*2 cups diced cucumber*
*1½ teaspoons salt*
*½ teaspoon pepper*
*1½ cups salad dressing*

In large bowl, mix potatoes, eggs, celery, onion, green pepper, pickles and cucumbers well. Add salt and pepper, then salad dressing and mix well. Refrigerate.

## CORNBREAD SALAD

*1 (8 x 8-inch) pan cornbread, crumbled*
*6 to 8 green onions with tops, chopped*
*6 radishes, sliced*
*½ green bell pepper*
*2 fresh tomatoes, diced*
*¼ cup mayonnaise*
*¼ cup cucumber dressing*
*2 teaspoons prepared mustard*

Combine cornbread, green onions, radishes, pepper and tomatoes. Mix mayonnaise, dressing and mustard. Pour over cornbread and toss. Chill and serve.

At our house we enjoy food, friends and family. We are comfortable serving beans (if they've simmered for two days), cornbread, a salad and dessert. Through the rodeo and political years we have learned one thing: Real food and good friends make a winning combination. (Donna McSpadden)

**All this eating raw, bloody, rare meat, like they order in big hotels— that's just city people— that ain't old western folks.**

—*Will Rogers*

∩

## MARTHA'S FAVORITE CHEESE SALAD

*1 (8-ounce) can crushed pineapple with juice*
*¼ cup sugar*
*1 (3-ounce) package lemon flavored gelatin*
*1 cup cold water*
*1 cup shredded cheddar cheese*
*½ cup chopped pecans*
*1 (20-ounce) container whipped topping*

Heat the pineapple with juice and add sugar and gelatin. After it is dissolved, add cold water and refrigerate. When it begins to gel, add cheese, nuts and fold in whipped topping. Mix well. Refrigerate until set. (Martha Gilliam)

## DIET CARROT SALAD

1 cup yogurt
1 tablespoon orange juice
2 tablespoons honey
2 cups diced carrots
½ cup raisins
1 large unpeeled apple, diced

Combine yogurt, orange juice and honey in medium bowl and blend well. Add carrots, raisins and apples and toss well. Chill. Makes 6 to 8 servings.

∩

## WALDORF SALAD

½ cup salad dressing
1 tablespoon lemon juice
1 tablespoon sugar
1½ cups diced, unpeeled, tart red apples
½ cup chopped celery
Lettuce
1 cup chopped walnuts

Combine salad dressing, lemon juice and sugar and toss with apples and celery. Arrange crisp, chilled lettuce on salad plates and spoon salad over lettuce. Sprinkle with nuts. Makes 6 servings.

∩

## NIFTY FOR TWO APPLE SALAD

1 large, cold apple, chopped
1 large, rib celery, chopped
½ cup chopped pecans
¼ cup Miracle Whip

Mix all ingredients, chill and serve.
(Carolyn Deffenbaugh)

## SPECIAL JELLO SALAD

*1 (3-ounce) package lime flavored gelatin*
*1 (8-ounce) can crushed pineapple*
*½ cup cold water*
*1 package dry Dream Whip*
*1 (8-ounce) carton small curd cottage cheese*
*1 cup mini-marshmallows*
*½ cup chopped pecans*
*½ cup chopped maraschino cherries*

In saucepan, combine gelatin, pineapple (undrained) and water and boil 3 minutes. Put in refrigerator until set. Prepare Dream Whip according to package directions. Add gelatin, cottage cheese, marshmallows, pecans and cherries to whipped cream and mix well. Fold in with gelatin and pour into mold. Refrigerate until set.

Ω

## TEXAS CLOUD BURST

*1 (3-ounce) package lemon-flavored gelatin*
*1 cup boiling water*
*1 cup grated cheese*
*1 (8-ounce) can crushed pineapple, drained*
*1 cup whipping cream, whipped*

Combine gelatin and water. Chill until slightly thickened. Fold in cheese, pineapple and whipped cream. Pour into 1-quart mold. Chill. Makes 6 servings.

**If you let women have their way, you will generally get even with them in the end.**

*-Will Rogers*

## MILLIONAIRE SALAD

*1 (3-ounce) package lemon flavored gelatin*
*1 cup pineapple tidbits*
*1 cup mandarin oranges*
*1 cup shredded coconut*
*1 cup chopped pecans*
*1 cup miniature marshmallows*
*1 cup sour cream*

Prepare gelatin according to package directions, chill and cut into cubes. Mix together pineapple, oranges, coconut, pecans and marshmallows, mix well then add sour cream. Fold in gelatin and stir just to mix, being careful not to break up the gelatin. Chill and serve.

**A slogan says, 'Two can live as cheap as one.' Why, two can't even live as cheap as two, much less one.**

—*Will Rogers*

∩

## PARADISE CINNAMON SALAD

*⅓ cup cinnamon candies*
*1 (6-ounce) package lemon flavored gelatin*
*2 cups boiling water*
*2 cups applesauce*
*2 (3-ounce) packages cream cheese, softened*
*¼ cup cream*
*2 tablespoons salad dressing*

Dissolve candies and gelatin in water, then stir in applesauce. Chill until partially set. Pour into (8-inch) square bowl. Mix cream cheese, cream and salad dressing until smooth. Stir gently into applesauce mixture for swirled effect. Chill until firm. Serve squares on greens. Makes 9 to 12 servings.

# COCA-CRANBERRYBANANA MOLD

1 (3-ounce) package raspberry flavored gelatin
1 cup boiling water
1 (1-pound) can whole cranberry sauce
2 bananas, sliced
½ cup chopped pecans

Dissolve gelatin in water. Add cranberry sauce and stir until blended. Chill until partially thickened. Add bananas and pecans. Spoon into molds. Chill until firm. Serve on greens. Makes 6 to 9 servings.

Ω

# COLA CHERRY SALAD

1 (20-ounce) can crushed pineapple
1 (29-ounce) can Bing cherries, seeded
1 (3-ounce) package raspberry flavored gelatin
1 (3-ounce) package strawberry flavored gelatin
1 (8-ounce) package cream cheese, softened
1 cup chopped nuts
1 cup Coca-Cola

Reserve juice from pineapple and cherries to equal 2 cups. Add water if necessary. Heat juice to boiling point. Add raspberry and strawberry gelatin and stir until dissolved. Chill until syrupy. Mash cream cheese with fork and add to gelatin. Add fruit, nuts and Coca-Cola and chill. Makes a large dish.

**There is nothing as stupid as an educated man if you get him off the thing he was educated in.**

—*Will Rogers*

## GRANDMOTHER'S COLA SALAD

*1 (10½-ounce) can dark Bing cherries, drained*
*1 (4-ounce) can crushed pineapple, drained*
*2 (3-ounce) packages cherry flavored gelatin*
*12 ounces Pepsi*
*1 cup chopped nuts*
*1 package cream cheese, softened*

Add cherries, pineapple and gelatin to saucepan and heat until gelatin is dissolved. Cool and add Pepsi, then refrigerate until it starts to congeal. Add nuts and cream cheese and mix well. Refrigerate until set. Makes 12 servings. (Les and Martha Gillian, entertainer)

∩

## DELICIOUS BUTTERMILK SALAD

*1 (15½-ounce) can crushed pineapple*
*1 large package apricot flavored gelatin*
*2 cups buttermilk*
*1 (20-ounce) carton whipped topping*
*½ cup chopped pecans*

Heat pineapple with juice and gelatin to boiling point and let cool. When it starts to gel, fold in buttermilk, whipped topping and pecans. Chill.

## DELITEFUL
## ORANGE–PINEAPPLE SALAD

*1 (8-ounce) can crushed pineapple*
*1 (3-ounce) package orange flavored gelatin*
*1 (3-ounce) package cream cheese, softened*
*1 cup whipping cream, whipped*
*1 carrot, grated*

Drain pineapple, reserve juice. Add water to juice to make 1 cup and heat to boiling. Add liquid to gelatin and cream cheese to mixture and beat until smooth. Cool, stirring occasionally. Fold in whipping cream, carrots, pineapple and cooled gelatin. Pour into individual molds and chill until firm. Makes 8 to 12 servings.

Ω

## SIDE-KICK CRANBERRY SALAD

*2 cups cranberries*
*1 cup water*
*1 cup sugar*
*1 package cherry flavored gelatin*
*1 ½ cups miniature marshmallows*
*1 cup diced celery*
*1 cup chopped apples*
*1 cup chopped pecans*
*Whipping cream, whipped*

Cook cranberries, sugar and water until cranberries pop open. Add gelatin and stir until dissolved. Remove from heat and add marshmallows. Stir until dissolved. Chill until starting to gel and add celery, apples and pecans. Chill and top with whipped cream.

> The good old days with most of us was when we didn't earn enough to pay an income tax.
>
> —Will Rogers

## COLORADO FREEZE SALAD

2 (3-ounce) packages cream cheese, softened
Juice of ½ lemon
½ cup sugar
1 (10-ounce) carton frozen strawberries, thawed
1 cup miniature marshmallows
2 bananas, diced
1 cup cream, whipped

To cream cheese add lemon juice and sugar mixing well. Add all other ingredients, folding in whipping cream last. Freeze overnight before serving.

## YUM YUM FRUIT SALAD

2 (20-ounce) cans crushed pineapple
⅓ cup sugar
2 tablespoons flour
2 eggs, lightly beaten
¼ cup orange juice
3 tablespoons lemon juice
1 tablespoon vegetable oil
2 (17-ounce) cans fruit cocktail, drained
2 (11-ounce) cans mandarin oranges, drained
1 banana, sliced
1 (20-ounce) carton whipped topping

Drain pineapple, reserving 1-cup juice in a small saucepan; set aside. To saucepan add sugar, flour, egg, orange juice, lemon juice and oil. Bring to a boil, stirring constantly. Boil for 1 minute. Remove from heat and let cool. In salad bowl, combine mixture with pineapple, reserved pineapple juice, fruit cocktail, oranges and banana. Fold in whipped topping. Chill for several hours. Makes 12 to 16 servings.

## CRANBERRY FLUFF

2 cups raw cranberries, ground
3 cups miniature marshmallows
¾ cup sugar
2 cups diced, unpared, tart apples
½ cup seedless green grapes
½ cup coarsely chopped pecans
¼ teaspoon salt
1 cup whipping cream, whipped
Lettuce

Combine cranberries, marshmallows and sugar. Cover and chill overnight. Add apples, grapes, pecans and salt. Fold in whipping cream. Chill and serve in lettuce cups. Garnish with a cluster of green grapes, if desired. Makes 8 to 10 servings.

∩

## CELEBRATE SALAD

1 (8-ounce) package cream cheese, softened
¼ cup sour cream
2 tablespoons confectioner's sugar
1 tablespoon lemon juice
¼ teaspoon salt
½ cup orange sections
½ cup chopped walnuts
2 cups diced bananas
1 cup whipped cream
½ cup maraschino cherries, halved

Beat cream cheese, sour cream, lemon juice and salt until light and fluffy. Fold in remaining ingredients. Scoop into shallow mold and chill.

I'll bet you the time ain't far off when a woman won't know anymore than a man.

—Will Rogers

## HOLLANDAISE SAUCE

½ cup butter
2 egg yolks
Dash cayenne pepper
¼ teaspoon salt
½ cup boiling water
1 tablespoon lemon juice

Cream butter, add egg yolks, dash of pepper and salt. Add boiling water and stir until right consistency. Add lemon juice, stirring rapidly. Serve with asparagus, broccoli or fish.

Ω

## FARMERS RANCH DRESSING

¾ cup mayonnaise
¼ cup buttermilk
⅓ cup minced celery
2 tablespoons chopped parsley
1 tablespoon grated onion
1 clove garlic, crushed
¼ teaspoon dried thyme
¼ teaspoon celery seed
¼ teaspoon salt
⅛ teaspoon ground pepper

In medium bowl, combine all ingredients and mix well. Cover and refrigerate until ready to use.

## BLUE CHEESE DRESSING

*3 ounces blue cheese, crumbled*
*1 cup sour cream*
*1 cup salad dressing*
*2 teaspoons soy sauce*
*1 clove garlic, minced*
*¼ teaspoon salt*
*Juice of 1 lemon*
*Dash vinegar*

Mix all ingredients and chill 2 hours before serving.
Makes 2 cups.

∩

## THOUSAND ISLAND DRESSING

*1 cup salad dressing*
*½ cup catsup*
*2 tablespoons sweet relish*
*1 hard-boiled egg, finely chopped*

In bowl, combine all ingredients and chill before
serving. Makes 1½ cups.

∩

## FRENCH DRESSING

*1 (10¾-ounce) can tomato soup*
*1 cup salad oil*
*¼ cup sugar*
*½ cup vinegar*
*Dash garlic salt*
*Salt*
*Dash paprika*

In large bowl, mix all ingredients and pour into a 1-
quart fruit jar and shake. Chill. Makes 3 cups.

**There's nothing will upset a state economic condition like the legislature. It's better to have termites in your house than the legislature.**

—*Will Rogers*

## POPPY SEED DRESSING

*1 cup sugar*
*½ cup vinegar*
*2 teaspoons salt*
*2 teaspoons dried mustard*
*2 cups salad oil*
*1 small onion, grated*
*1 tablespoon poppy seeds*
*Dash cayenne pepper*

In medium bowl, combine all ingredients and chill. Makes 2 cups.

**A politician is just like a pickpocket; it's almost impossible to get one to reform.**

—*Will Rogers*

∩

## HONEY DRESSING

*½ cup sugar*
*1 teaspoon dried mustard*
*1 teaspoon paprika*
*1 teaspoon celery seeds*
*⅓ cup honey*
*⅓ cup salad oil*
*1 small onion, grated*
*1 tablespoon lemon juice*
*1 cup oil*
*¼ teaspoon salt*

Mix ingredients in blender. Serve over salad greens. This is also delicious over fresh fruit.

## CAN'T CRITICIZE BAKED BEANS

*2½ cups dried beans*
*2 tablespoons molasses*
*2 tablespoons brown sugar*
*1 tablespoon salt*
*¾ teaspoon mustard*
*3½ cups boiling water*
*3 ounces salt pork or bacon*

Wash beans and add enough cold water to cover beans. Cover, let stand at least 6 hours. Drain water in which the beans were soaked. Add molasses, brown sugar, salt, mustard and boiling water to the beans and place pan over low heat until mixture reaches the boiling point. Add pork or bacon and pour into a baking dish. Cover and bake at 250° for 6 hours.

∩

## MRS. ROGERS' SOUTHERN GREEN BEANS

*2 pounds string beans*
*½ pound salt pork*
*1 quart water*
*1 onion, chopped*
*Salt*
*Pepper*

Cut beans approximately 1½-inches in length. Cube and brown salt pork. Bring water to a boil and add beans, salt pork, onion, salt and pepper. Simmer slowly about 2 to 3 hours.

**Saw in the paper where four innocent people were shot in New York City in one day. That's amazing. It's hard to find four innocent people in New York City.**

*—Will Rogers*

**[87]**

## COMPANY GREEN BEANS

*1 pound fresh green beans*
*¼ cup butter*
*½ cup hazelnuts, toasted, chopped*
*1 tablespoon lemon juice*
*1 teaspoon fresh parsley*
*½ teaspoon dried basil*
*½ teaspoon salt*

In saucepan, cover beans with water and cook covered until crisp-tender. In small saucepan over medium-high heat, melt butter and heat thoroughly with hazelnuts, lemon juice, parsley, basil and salt. Drain beans, add butter mixture and toss to coat. Serve immediately. Makes 4 servings.

∩

## CRISP 5-MINUTE CABBAGE

*1½ cups milk*
*4 cups shredded cabbage*
*1½ tablespoons flour*
*1½ tablespoons butter, melted*
*1 teaspoon salt*
*⅛ teaspoon pepper*

Simmer milk and cabbage about 5 minutes. Mix flour and butter and stir in hot milk a little at a time. Stir the mixture constantly and cook 4-5 minutes or until thickened. Season with salt and pepper. Makes 4 servings.

**The Democrats are investigating the Republican slush fund. And if they find where it's coming from, they want theirs.**

—*Will Rogers*

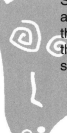

## GRANDMA WILSON'S CABBAGE

1 head cabbage
¼ cup butter
1 cup hot water
2 slices bacon
Salt
Pepper

In skillet, put all ingredients and cook slowly until tender. Stir occasionally. Salt and pepper to taste and serve.

∩

## FRIED CAULIFLOWER

8 cups cauliflower flowerets
4 eggs
1 teaspoon parsley
1 teaspoon garlic salt
1 teaspoon salt
Paprika
2 cups breadcrumbs
4 tablespoons oil
Dash pepper

Boil cauliflower for 10 minutes until tender and drain. In bowl, combine eggs, parsley, garlic salt, salt and pepper and mix well. Dip cauliflower into mixture and coat with breadcrumbs. In skillet add oil and heat. Cook cauliflower until brown. Drain on paper towel. Place on plate and garnish with paprika. Makes 6 servings.

**Nice, France, is pronounced "neece" not "nice"! They have no word for nice in French.**

—Will Rogers

## ORANGE GLAZED CARROTS

¼ cup butter, melted
1 tablespoon sugar
1 cup orange juice
1 pound carrots, peeled, sliced

Combine all ingredients in a saucepan; cover and simmer 15 to 20 minutes or until carrots are tender. Uncover and cook until liquid is absorbed. Makes 4 to 6 servings.

Ω

## CARROT RELISH

4 cups diced carrots
4 cups diced green tomatoes
2 cups diced onions
1 cup packed brown sugar
2 cups vinegar
1 tablespoon salt
2 tablespoons mixed spices

Cook carrots until tender, add remaining ingredients and cook 30 minutes. Cool and put in jars.

Ω

## IOWA CORN WITH A LIFT

1 (10-ounce) package frozen whole kernel corn
¼ cup butter or margarine
1 tablespoon brown sugar
2 tablespoons whiskey
⅓ cup chopped pecans

Cook and stir corn in butter in 10-inch skillet over medium heat until tender. Stir in brown sugar and whiskey. Cook uncovered, stirring constantly, until mixture thickens, about 2 minutes. Sprinkle with pecans. Makes 4 servings.

## FRESH FROZEN CORN

*8 cups fresh corn*
*½ stick butter or margarine*
*3 tablespoons sugar*
*Water*

Cut corn from cob and mix with butter, sugar and enough water to keep corn from sticking to pot. Bring to a boil. Stir often, cool and put in plastic bags and freeze.

Ω

## OKIES FRIED CORN

*1 (15-ounce) can, whole kernel corn, drained*
*1 egg, beaten*
*1 tablespoon flour*
*½ teaspoon salt*
*½ teaspoon sugar*
*¼ cup butter*

Combine all ingredients except butter and mix well. Drop by spoonful into moderately hot pan with butter. Brown carefully on both sides. Reduce heat and cook gently on both sides. May be served with meat course or as a dessert with confectioners sugar.

Ω

## OLD SOUTHERN GRITS

*4 cups water*
*1 cup grits*
*1 teaspoon salt*
*1 tablespoon butter*

Bring salted water to a boil. Add grits slowly so that boiling does not stop. Add butter and cover and let cook 40 minutes on low. Stir often. Serve hot with butter. Makes 4 servings.

> **So much money is being spent on the campaigns that I doubt if either man, as good as they are, are worth what it will cost to elect them.**
> —*Will Rogers*

**[91]**

## CAN'T FAIL CORN PUDDING

*2 eggs*
*1 (15-ounce) can cream-style corn*
*⅓ cup sugar*
*2 tablespoons flour*
*½ cup milk*
*½ teaspoon salt*
*½ teaspoon nutmeg*
*2 tablespoons butter, melted*

In medium bowl, beat eggs slightly, then add corn, sugar, flour, milk, slat and nutmeg and mix well. Pour into greased 1½-quart baking dish. Pour butter over mixture and bake at 350° for 1½ hours.

**They call it the Latin Quarter because nobody speaks Latin, and nobody has a quarter.**

—*Will Rogers*

Ω

## SKILLET FRIED OKRA

*1 cup yellow cornmeal*
*½ cup flour*
*1½ teaspoons salt*
*¼ teaspoon pepper*
*¾ cup fresh okra, cut in ½-inch pieces*
*¼ cup bacon drippings*

In medium bowl, combine cornmeal, flour, salt and pepper. Add okra and toss until well coated. In a 10-inch skillet heat enough bacon drippings to cover bottom of skillet. Add some okra and cook, turning frequently, until crispy and brown. Drain on paper towel. Repeat, adding more bacon drippings as needed.

## FRIED BANANA PEPPERS

*6 banana peppers*
*1½ cups water*
*1 cup milk*
*1 cup flour*
*Oil*

Split peppers and, remove seeds. Let set in cold water 10 minutes. Remove from water and put in milk. Let set for 10 minutes. Roll in flour, return to milk and dip, then roll again in flour. Deep fry until golden brown.

∩

## YUM YUM POTATO PUFFS

*¾ cup water*
*¼ cup margarine or butter*
*1 teaspoon instant minced onion*
*⅛ teaspoon salt*
*1 cup instant mashed potatoes*
*¼ cup flour*
*2 eggs*
*Sour cream, optional*
*Green onions, optional*

Heat water, butter, onion and salt to boil in 1½-quart saucepan. Stir in potatoes and flour. Stir vigorously over low heat just until mixture forms a ball, about 1 minute. Remove from heat. Beat in eggs until smooth. Drop dough by heaping tablespoonful onto ungreased cookie sheet. Bake at 400° until puffed and golden, about 30 minutes. Serve with sour cream and green onions.

**The Republicans want a man that can lend dignity to the office, and the Democrats want a man that will lend some money.**

—*Will Rogers*

**[93]**

## POTATO CORN FLAKE SLICES

*4 potatoes, cut into ¼-inch slices*
*2 tablespoons margarine or butter, melted*
*½ cup finely crushed corn flakes*
*1 teaspoon salt*

Place potato slices on greased cookie sheet and brush with butter. Mix cereal and salt, then sprinkle over potatoes. Cook uncovered at 375° until tender and golden brown. Makes 4 to 6 servings.

∩

## SINFUL MASHED POTATOES

*2 pounds small red potatoes, quartered*
*Water*
*½ cup heavy cream*
*½ cup butter*
*1 teaspoon salt*

In a large saucepan, cover potatoes with water and bring to a boil. Lower heat and simmer until potatoes are soft. Drain and mash potatoes before returning to saucepan. Over very low heat, gradually add cream, butter and salt. Makes 6 servings.

∩

## SKILLET CANDIED SWEET POTATOES

*1 cup packed brown sugar*
*¼ cup butter*
*¼ cup water*
*½ teaspoon salt*
*6 cooked sweet potatoes*

Mix brown sugar, butter, water and salt and cook until mixture boils. Add sweet potatoes and cook in skillet slowly, turning occasionally, about 20 minutes or until potatoes have caramel-like glaze. Makes 6 servings.

# HOLIDAY SWEET POTATOES

*3 cups cooked, sweet potatoes*
*2 eggs, beaten*
*½ cup milk*
*1 cup sugar*
*1 cup coconut*
*1 teaspoon vanilla*
*1 cup packed brown sugar*
*1 cup chopped pecans*
*⅓ cup flour*
*⅓ cup butter, softened*

In bowl, mash sweet potatoes and mix in egg, milk, sugar, coconut and vanilla to blend. Put in 2 quart baking dish. In medium bowl, mix brown sugar, pecans, flour and butter. Mix well then crumble over sweet potato mixture. Bake at 350° for 30 minutes.

Ω

# SWEET POTATO CAKES

*1 cup cooked, mashed sweet potatoes*
*½ cup milk*
*½ cup oil*
*Flour*
*2 teaspoons baking powder*
*1½ teaspoon salt*
*1½ teaspoon sugar*

Preheat oven to 425°. In large bowl, combine sweet potatoes and stir in milk and oil. Sift together flour and dry ingredients in separate bowl. Add dry ingredients to the potato mixture and mix lightly until dough holds together. Knead gently on floured board. Roll out to ¼-inch thick and cut as you would biscuits. Bake on cookie sheet at 350° for 10 to 20 minutes. (Cherokee National Historical Society)

They only hold political conventions every four years cause it takes that long to get a straight face from the last one.

—Will Rogers

[95]

## TWICE-BAKED YAMS

*6 sweet potatoes*
*Oil*
*¼ cup sour cream*
*¼ cup milk*
*2 tablespoons margarine or butter, melted*
*2 tablespoons brown sugar*
*⅛ teaspoon salt*

**The Oklahomans that move to California raise the IQ of both places.**

*—Will Rogers*

Rub skins of sweet potatoes with oil and prick with fork to allow steam to escape. Cook at 375° oven until tender, 35 to 45 minutes. Slice lengthwise. Scoop out inside, leaving a thin shell. Mash potatoes until no lumps remain. Beat in sour cream and milk. Beat in butter, brown sugar and salt until light and fluffy. Place shells in ungreased baking dish and fill with potato mixture. Bake uncovered at 400° until filling is golden, about 20 minutes.

Ω

## CUCUMBER RELISH

*2 cups vinegar*
*3 cups sugar*
*4 sweet peppers*
*4 large onions, chopped*
*8 cups chopped cucumbers*
*1 teaspoon turmeric*
*2 teaspoons celery seed*
*1 teaspoon cinnamon*
*Salt*

Bring vinegar and sugar to a boil. Add remaining ingredients and boil for 20 minutes. Put in jars.

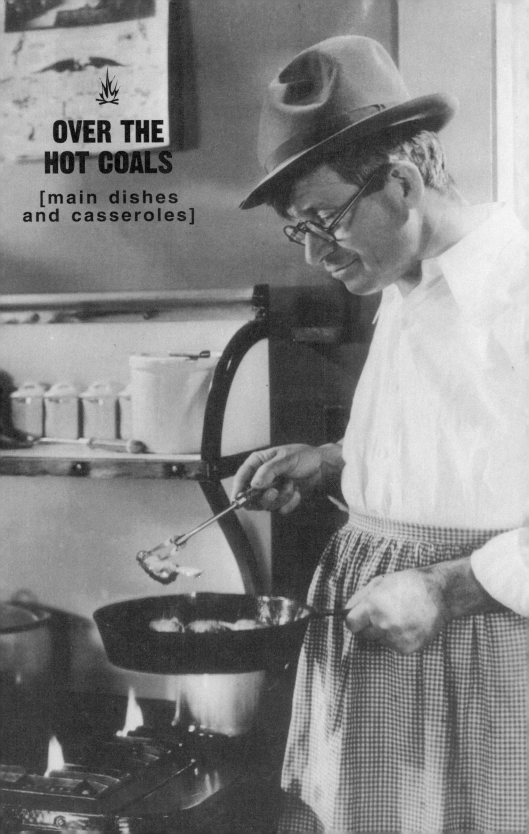

# OVER THE HOT COALS

[main dishes and casseroles]

# THE STAR

**(left to right) Douglas Fairbanks, Will Rogers, Tom Mix, and Rob Wagner**

Will Rogers' first big break in show business came a Madison Square Garden in New York when he was working with Colonel Zack Mulhall's Wild West Show. A long-horned steer jumped from the arena floor into the stands. As the crowd scattered, Will roped the steer and helped prevent anyone from getting injured. The invaluable publicity he received helped him start his vaudeville career.

In *State Fair* the plot centered around a prize boar known as Blue Boy. When the filming was completed, Will was asked if he would like to buy Blue Boy; there was a lot of meat for the Rogers' family. Will paused and said, "No, I can't do it. I wouldn't feel right eatin' a fellow actor."

*A Connecticut Yankee* for Fox Studios was in black and white. When Myrna Loy kissed Will Rogers in the film, he had to blush. The only way this could be done was to hand tint each frame progressively darker pink. This had to be done on every print sent out.

Twentieth Century Fox dedicated a new modern sound stage to Will Rogers. The plaque showed a likeness of Will and had these words:
"This stage we dedicate to your memory, Will Rogers, you who made the world laugh and made the world love you."

**Will Rogers and Tom Mix knew each other from the days of the famed 101 Ranch. They worked together in the Zeigfeld Follies and both went on to become major motion picture stars.**

Will Rogers didn't read his script, but would come on the set and ask, "What's this

**Bill "Bojangles" Robinson teaches Will Rogers to tap dance in the movie *In Old Kentucky*.**

next scene all about?" We would talk it over, he would ask, "Do I have any lines?" I'd say, "I'm afraid so." He'd say, "Well let me look at 'em." I'd tell him, " Go on, change them, say it in you own words." He would go away muttering, come back and say the lines in typical Rogers fashion, which was better than any writer could write for him.

*—John Ford, Director*

**In 1934 Will Rogers was the number one box office attraction in motion pictures, beating out such stars as Clark Gable and Spencer Tracey. In 1935 he finished second to Shirley Temple.**

As a young actor Joel McCrea was cast in Fox's movie, *Lightnin'*, starring Will Rogers. Joel had a scene with Will, both in a buggy. Since Will ad-libbed his lines, McCrea had no idea when to say his lines. Will said, "Joe, you're just a cowboy, and I'm gonna' help you. I change the dialogue, sometimes I improve it, sometimes I don't. When I think I've said enough, I'll stop, and then I'll poke you and then you can talk".

Will Rogers made his first motion picture in Ft. Lee, New Jersey, in 1918, while still working in the Follies. It was *Laughing Bill Hyde*. He eventually became the highest paid actor in the movies.

When Will Rogers began work in *Doubting Thomas,* he discovered his Fox bosses

Joe E. Brown,
Will Rogers,
Eddie Cantor,
unidentified.

had engaged a valet for him. Will put up with the whisk-brooming and tie straightening the first day with only passive restraint, but on the following morning the servant was conspicuously absent. Investigation revealed that Will was paying the fellow five dollars extra a day to make himself scarce.

A three-year-old child obviously doesn't know anything about acting schools, yet they are the greatest actors in the world. That's exactly the way Will Rogers was. He just had an instinct, and he followed that instinct that prompted him every minute through everything he did. That is to me the highest and greatest form of acting there is. Rogers was probably the beginning of the school, "Don't try to act, be it."

Will Rogers in polo attire in front of dressing rooms on the Fox Studios lot.

—*Henry King, Director* State Fair

[101]

**John Ford, legendary movie director, and Will Rogers.**

Will Rogers movie contract with Fox Studios called for three or four motion pictures per year. He wanted to do them consecutively so he could get them done in the shortest time possible, leaving him free to travel and pursue his other interests. He liked to complete one movie and immediately start on the next one.

Steamboat Round the Bend was released nine days after Will Rogers' death. The final scene was changed. When it was made the closing scene showed Will waving to Irvin S. Cobb as Cobb's boat faded out of the picture. The last thing one saw was Will waving farewell. Everyone would have felt that Will was waving farewell to the world and to them. The scene was eliminated because they did not want audiences leaving the theater crying.

In a movie scene with Will Rogers I had to carry a chicken down the street. It was flapping its wings and kicking hard. Will looked at me and said, "You know, you're holding it the wrong way. If you hold it the right way, you won't have any trouble." I asked him, "What is the right way?" Will answered innocently, "I haven't any idea."

— *Sterling Holloway, Actor*

Will Rogers scorned make-up and never took

acting classes, but he was the hottest star

for a decade in the Ziegfeld Follies and in 71 movies: 50 silents and 21 talkies.

Will Rogers was experienced in many facets of motion pictures, and decided to produce his own silent films. He produced *A Ropin' Fool*, *Fruits of Faith*, and *One Day in 365*. They were well received critically, but the large studios controlled distribution, and Will lost all his savings and family assets. He went on the lecture circuit and became the most celebrated after-dinner speaker in New York City, getting fees of $1,000 to $1,500 per engagement. He repaid every penny of the accumulated debts.

Hattie McDaniel (known best from *Gone With the Wind* and four other ladies are joined by Will Rogers in singing "My Old Kentucky Home" in Fox Film Corporation's *Judge Priest* in 1934.

Will Rogers and Flo Ziegfeld never had a contract. They worked on a handshake all the years Will was with the Follies. In one of the early Follies, Will sent in and said, "Mr. Ziegfeld, when I left Oklahoma I promised my wife and children that some day I'd make $500 a week. If I ever make that the dream of my life would be fulfilled." Ziegfeld promptly fulfilled his dream, but the following season Will asked for $600. "What's the big idea?" asked the famous producer. "I thought you wife and children were perfectly satisfied with $500." "They are," replied Will, "but since then we have another child and he's kicking!"

—As told by Eddie Cantor, comedian and actor

**Will Rogers in *David Harum*.**

## WILL ROGERS' "GOOD OL' OKLAHOMA BEANS"

*2 pounds small white navy beans*
*1 generous ham hock*
*1 onion, peeled*
*Salt*
*Pepper*

Soak beans overnight in cold water. In the morning, drain and cover with fresh water. Bring to boil and add ham hock, onion, salt and pepper. Simmer slowly for 4 hours. Add more water, if necessary so beans will be kind of soupy. Each serving should include a portion of ham. (Will Rogers)

∩

## BEAN DUMPLINGS

**Only a fool argues with a skunk, a mule or a cook.**

—*Will Rogers*

*2 cups dried pinto beans*
*4 cups cornmeal*
*½ cup all-purpose flour*
*1 teaspoon baking soda*
*1 teaspoon salt*

Cook beans in water until tender. Mix together cornmeal, flour, baking soda and salt. Add cooked beans to dry ingredients with slotted spoon, reserving bean soup. Add enough bean soup to mixture to form a stiff dough. Roll in balls and drop into a pot of boiling water. Let cook for 30 minutes at a slow boil. (Cherokee National Historical Society)

## WILL'S CHILI AND BEANS

*1 pound round steak, chopped*
*1 onion, chopped*
*Salt*
*1 (15-ounce) can tomatoes*
*1 (4-ounce) can chopped pimientos*
*2 (15-ounce) cans red kidney beans, drained*

Sauté steak and onion until brown. Add tomatoes, pimientos and salt. Cook 1 hour, then add kidney beans or soak 2 cups dried red kidney beans overnight and cook over very slow fire. (Will Rogers)

Ω

## COWPOKE CHILI

*2½ pounds ground beef*
*1 large onion, chopped*
*2 tablespoons cumin*
*2 tablespoons garlic powder*
*2 tablespoons oregano*
*½ cup paprika*
*1 cup chili powder*
*2 cups water*
*½ tablespoon pepper*
*1 tablespoon salt*
*1 cup flour*

Brown meat and drain. Simmer with all ingredients except flour for 1 hour. Combine flour and water and mix well. Pour flour mixture a little at a time into chili to get desired thickness. Simmer at least 30 minutes. Makes 12 to 15 servings.

**The way to judge a good comedy is by how long it will last and have people talk about it. Now Congress has turned out some that have lived for years and people are still laughin' about 'em.**

—Will Rogers

## COWPUNCHER BEEF CHILI

*2 cups chopped beef, cooked*
*1 (8-ounce) jar salsa*
*¼ cups chopped green onions*
*1 tablespoon chili powder*
*1 (15-ounce) can kidney beans, drained*
*½ cup shredded cheddar cheese*

In medium saucepan, combine beef, salsa, onion and chili powder. Bring to a boil and reduce heat to low. Cover tightly and simmer 10 minutes. Stir in beans and heat through. Serve with cheese. Makes 4 servings.

Ω

## JAMES WHITMORE'S CHILI WITH AN ATTITUDE

*2 pounds ground beef*
*1 small onion, chopped*
*½ tablespoon garlic*
*½ tablespoon chili powder*
*½ teaspoon ground red pepper*
*½ teaspoon pepper*
*½ teaspoon red chili pepper*
*1 (8-ounce) can tomatoes*
*1 tablespoon paprika*

Brown beef, drain and add onion and garlic. Simmer 15 minutes. Add remaining ingredients, cover and simmer for 2½ hours. Makes 6 to 8 servings.

**Lord, the money we do spend on Government and it's not one bit better than the government we got for one-third the money twenty years ago.**

—*Will Rogers*

## SIX-SHOOTER CHILI

*2 tablespoons chopped, green pepper*
*2 cloves garlic, minced*
*3½ tablespoons chopped onion*
*Oil*
*1 pound ground beef*
*2 tablespoons chili powder*
*1 (16-ounce) can tomatoes*
*1 (16-ounce) can pinto beans*

Cook green pepper, garlic and onion in oil until tender. Add ground beef, brown and drain. Add chili powder, tomatoes, beans and salt and simmer for 1 hour.

∩

## BELLYFUL CHILI

*1½ pounds ground beef*
*1 pound lean pork*
*1 (16-ounce) can tomatoes*
*1 teaspoon garlic powder*
*1 small onion, chopped*
*1 (10-ounce) can chopped green chilies*
*1 (16-ounce) can pinto beans*
*½ teaspoon salt*

Brown meat and add all ingredients, simmer 2 hours. Add water as needed.

**You have to have a serious streak in you or you can't see the funny side of the other fellow.**

*—Will Rogers*

## VEGETARIAN CHILI

*1 (16-ounce) can red beans*
*1 small onion, chopped*
*4 tablespoons chili mix*
*½ teaspoon garlic salt*
*1 (3-ounce) can diced tomatoes, drained*
*1 (3-ounce) can tomato purée*
*4 cups water*

Add all ingredients and simmer for 1½ hours. Add more water if needed.

## SAUERBRATEN A LA ELIZABETH
**Will Rogers Memorial, Gregory Malak, Curator**

*1 (4-pound) chuck roast*
*2½ cups vinegar*
*2 cups water*
*½ cup catsup*
*1 large onion, sliced*
*¼ cup packed brown sugar*
*¾ teaspoon ground cloves*
*Salt*
*Pepper*
*Cooked noodles*

Refrigerate and soak roast. Turn roast daily, in all ingredients except noodles for at least one week. Heat and bring to a boil, reduce temperature and simmer, covered until bubbly, about 1 to 2 hours. (Do not add any additional vinegar or water while cooking.) When meat is tender, take out and make gravy. Slice meat and return to gravy and heat. Serve over cooked noodles.

## WILL ROGERS, JR'S CORNED BEEF AND CABBAGE

1 (4–pound) corned beef brisket
Several whole pepper corns
1 bay leaf
1 to 2 heads of cabbage
White potatoes, boiled

Cover brisket with boiling water and seasonings. If only mildly corned, add 1 garlic clove. Simmer 4 hours until fork can penetrate to center. Wash and drain 1 to 2 heads firm cabbage and cut in wedges. Simmer on top of brisket the last 15 minutes of cooking. Serve with boiled, white potatoes

Ω

## COWBOY'S BEEF CASSEROLE

1 pound ground beef
2 eggs, beaten
1 cup self-rising cornmeal
1 (16-ounce) can cream-style corn
1 cup milk
¼ cup vegetable oil
2 cups shredded cheddar cheese
1 large onion, chopped
Pepper

Brown ground beef in large skillet and drain. Mix together cornmeal, cream-styled corn, milk and vegetable oil. Pour half the batter into a greased 10½-inch cast iron skillet or 10-inch deep-dish pie plate. Top evenly with ground beef followed by the cheese, onion and pepper. Pour remaining batter over the top. Bake at 350° for 45 to 55 minutes. Cut into wedges and serve. Makes 6 to 8 servings.

> Hollywood is like a desert water hole in Africa. Hang around long enough and every kind of animal in the world will drift in for refreshments.
>
> —Will Rogers

## STUFFED GREEN PEPPERS

*4 large green peppers*
*1 pound ground beef*
*1 large onion, chopped*
*1 tablespoon crushed garlic*
*¼ cup uncooked rice*
*1 tablespoon tomato paste*
*Salt*
*Pepper*
*½ cup water*
*2 tablespoons olive oil*

Cut tops off green peppers and remove seeds. Combine all other ingredients except oil and water. Stuff peppers with mixture. Arrange peppers in casserole dish with oil and water. Bake at 350° for 1 hour. Add more water, if needed. Makes 4 servings.

Ω

## WASH DAY CASSEROLE
### Will Rogers Memorial, Pat Lowe, Librarian

*1 pound ground beef*
*1 (15-ounce) can corn, drained*
*3 cups cooked macaroni and cheese*

Brown ground beef and drain. Put in baking dish then pour in corn with macaroni and cheese on top. Bake at 350° for 40 minutes. It's great.

**There are only two things I claim for myself in motion pictures. One is, I'm the ugliest man in them; second, I'm the only guy that's still got the same wife he started out with.**

—*Will Rogers*

## STEAK SUPPER IN FOIL

1 (1½-pound) chuck steak,
1-inch thick
1 (1½-ounce) envelope dehydrated onion
    soup mix
3 carrots, quartered
2 ribs celery, cut thinly
2 to 3 potatoes, quartered
2 tablespoons butter
½ teaspoon salt

Heat oven to 450°. Tear off 2½-foot length of 18-inch wide aluminum foil. Place steak in center and sprinkle with soup mix. Cover with vegetables. Dot vegetables with butter and sprinkle with salt. Fold foil over and seal securely to hold juices in. Place on baking sheet. Bake 1½ hours. Makes 4 servings.

∩

## LEFT-OVER ROAST BEEF STEW

2 cups cooked, cubed roast beef
2 red potatoes, cut into ¼-inch slices
⅔ cup water
1 teaspoon dried oregano leaves
½ teaspoon salt
1 cup frozen peas
2 tablespoons cornstarch
1 tablespoon lemon juice

In medium saucepan, combine beef, potatoes, water, oregano and salt. Bring to a boil then reduce heat to low. Cover tightly and simmer 10 to 12 minutes or until potatoes are tender. Stir in peas and heat through. Dissolve cornstarch in lemon juice and add to saucepan. Cook and stir until sauce is thickened and bubbly.

Let's be honest with ourselves and not take ourselves too serious, and never condemn the other fellow for doin' what we are doin' every day, only in a different way.

—Will Rogers

## MRS. O.B. LONG STEAK AND POTATOES

1½  pounds round steak, tenderized
½ cup flour
½ teaspoon salt
1 teaspoon pepper
¼ cup oil
3 cups sliced potatoes

Roll steak in flour, salt and pepper and brown in oil quickly on both sides. Lift and place sliced potatoes in skillet. Turn steak and cook slowly until potatoes are tender. (Dorothy Foster Bruffet)

∩

## SKILLET STROGANOFF

1 pound ground beef
1 onion, chopped
1 (10¾-ounce) can condensed beef broth
1 (4-ounce) can mushroom stems and pieces, drained
2 cups uncooked egg noodles
1½ cups water
¼ cup catsup
¼ teaspoon garlic powder
1 cup sour cream

Brown ground beef and onion in 10-inch skillet and drain. Stir in broth, mushrooms, noodles, water, catsup and garlic powder. Heat to boiling and reduce heat. Cover and simmer, stirring occasionally, until noodles are tender, about 30 minutes. A small amount of water can be added, if necessary. Stir in sour cream just before serving and heat just until hot.

# BUTTERMILK STROGANOFF

¼ cup flour
1 teaspoon salt
⅛ teaspoon pepper
¾ pound beef stew meat, cubed
2 tablespoons butter
¼ cup mushroom stems and pieces
1 cup chopped onions
¼ teaspoon garlic powder
1 cup water
1 teaspoon Worcestershire sauce
3 tablespoons catsup
¾ cup buttermilk
4 ounces noodles, cooked

Combine flour, salt and pepper and coat cubes of meat. In saucepan, melt butter, add meat and cook slowly until browned on all sides. Drain mushrooms and save liquor. Add onion, garlic powder, water, Worcestershire sauce, catsup and mushroom's liquor to meat. Cover and simmer until meat is tender, about 2 hours. Stir in mushrooms and buttermilk and heat only. Place noodles in ring around edge of serving bowl. Fill center with meat mixture.

> It's the fellow that knows when to quit that the audience wants more of.
> —*Will Rogers*

**[113]**

## LOUISIANA DIRTY RICE

*1 bell pepper, chopped*
*1 onion, chopped*
*1 stick margarine*
*1 (10¾-ounce) can onion soup*
*1 (10-ounce) can beef bouillon soup*
*1 (4-ounce) can mushrooms, drained*
*1 cup uncooked rice*

Sauté pepper and onion in margarine until tender. Mix all ingredients in 2-quart casserole dish. Cover and bake at 375° for 1 hour.

∩

## BEEF FRIED RICE

*¾ pound lean ground beef*
*6 green onions, chopped*
*3 large ribs celery, chopped*
*8 ounce bean sprouts*
*½ cup sliced mushrooms*
*½ cup finely chopped, red bell pepper*
*1 teaspoon grated fresh ginger*
*3 cups cooked rice*
*2 tablespoons soy sauce*
*Salt*
*Pepper*

Brown ground beef in large skillet and drain. Stir in onions, celery, bean sprouts, mushrooms, red bell pepper and ginger. Cook over medium high heat 5 minutes, stirring frequently. Stir in rice and soy sauce. Season with salt and pepper. Heat through, stirring occasionally. Makes 4 servings.

**Nowadays we take our comedians seriously and our politicians as a joke. It used to be the other way around.**

*—Will Rogers*

## CHICKEN-WILD RICE CASSEROLE

*2 cups cubed, cooked chicken*
*2 cups cooked wild rice*
*¼ cup chopped green pepper*
*1 (10¾-ounce) can cream of mushroom soup*
*½ soup can milk*
*Salt*
*Pepper*

Heat oven to 350°. Mix all ingredients together well. Place in greased, 2-quart baking dish. Bake 30 minutes. Makes 6 servings.

Ω

## CHICKEN AND SPINACH NOODLES

*1 (10-ounce) package spinach noodles*
*1 cup milk*
*2 (6¾-ounce) cans chunk chicken*
*1 (4-ounce) can mushroom stems and pieces, drained*
*1 small onion, finely chopped*
*¼ cup grated Romano cheese*
*2 tablespoons butter, melted*
*1 teaspoon pepper*

Cook noodles according to package directions and drain. Toss with remaining ingredients. Pour into ungreased, 2-quart casserole. Cover and cook at 350° until hot, about 30 minutes. Stir before serving.

**Hollywood: the Sodom and Gomorrah of the West.**

—*Will Rogers*

## SKILLET CHICKEN AND RICE

*1 tablespoon margarine*
*1 pound skinless, boneless chicken*
    *breasts, cut up*
*1 (10¾-ounce) can cream of mushroom soup*
*1 cup milk*
*1 tablespoon onion flakes*
*¼ teaspoon dried thyme*
*⅛ teaspoon pepper*
*2 cups frozen, cut green beans*
*2 cups uncooked, instant rice*

In large skillet melt margarine. Add chicken and cook until browned, stirring often. Remove and set aside. Add soup, milk, onion, thyme, pepper and beans and stir to combine. Heat to boil. Return chicken to pan. Cover and cook over low heat 5 minutes or until chicken is done. Add rice. Cover and remove from heat. Let stand 5 minutes. Makes 4 servings.

## CHICKEN A LA KING

*¼ cup butter*
*3 tablespoons flour*
*1 cup milk*
*2 cups diced, cooked chicken*
*1 (3-ounce) can sliced mushrooms, drained*
*¼ cup chopped pimiento, drained*
*1 cup chicken broth*
*1 teaspoon salt*
*Hot biscuits*

Blend butter, flour and milk together and cook, stirring constantly, over heat until sauce is thick. Add the remaining ingredients. Heat to boil. Serve over hot biscuits.

## EASY CHICKEN AND NOODLES

1 (10¾-ounce) can cream of chicken soup
½ cup milk
¾ cup grated Parmesan cheese
½ teaspoon pepper
2 cups cubed, cooked chicken
3 cups cooked, medium noodles

In large saucepan, heat all ingredients over medium heat, stirring occasionally. Makes 4 servings.

Ω

## DELICIOUS CHICKEN AND ASPARAGUS

1½ pounds fresh asparagus spears, halved
4 boneless, skinless chicken breasts
2 tablespoons cooking oil
½ teaspoon salt
¼ teaspoon pepper
1 (10¾-ounce) can condensed cream of
    chicken soup
½ cup mayonnaise
1 teaspoon lemon juice
½ teaspoon curry powder
1 cup shredded cheddar cheese

Partially cook the asparagus and drain. Place asparagus in greased 9-inch square baking dish. In skillet over medium heat, brown the chicken in oil on both sides. Season with salt and pepper and arrange chicken over asparagus. In a bowl, mix soup, mayonnaise, lemon and curry powder, then pour over chicken. Cover and bake at 375° for 45 minutes. Sprinkle with cheese. Let stand 5 minutes before serving. Makes 4 servings.

Like all the other comedians there in the Follies, I just came out to kill time while the gals changed from nothing to nothing.

—Will Rogers

**[117]**

## BARBECUED CHICKEN AND STUFFING

¼ cup catsup

2 tablespoons vinegar

2 tablespoons water

1½ teaspoons Worcestershire sauce

½ teaspoon chili powder

½ teaspoon dried mustard

2 cups diced, cooked chicken

2 cups baked bread stuffing

Combine catsup, vinegar, water, Worcestershire sauce, chili powder and dried mustard. Place chicken and half of the barbecue sauce into bottom of a 1-quart casserole dish. Top with stuffing. Slowly pour remaining sauce over stuffing. Bake at 350° for 30 minutes. Makes 6 servings.

**The American people are generous and will forgive about any weakness with the exception of stupidity.**

*—Will Rogers*

∩

## TURKEY-CHICKEN-CHOPS BREAD STUFFING

5 cups breadcrumbs

¼ cup diced onion

¼ cup diced celery

⅓ teaspoon salt

Dash pepper

½ teaspoon poultry seasoning

2 eggs

½ cup hot poultry broth

¼ cup chicken soup

½ cup minced parsley

Place all ingredients in large bowl and blend thoroughly. Place mixture in baking dish and bake at 350° for 30 to 35 minutes. (Can use 2 chicken bouillon cubes dissolved in ½ cup hot water instead of chicken soup.)

## CHICKEN SPOON BREAD CASSEROLE

¾ *cup cornmeal*
2 *tablespoons flour*
1 *teaspoon salt*
4 *cups chicken broth*
¼ *cup margarine*
4 *egg yolks, beaten*
3 *cups chopped, cooked chicken*
¼ *cup chopped onion*
4 *egg whites, beaten*

Combine cornmeal, flour and salt in heavy saucepan. Add broth, stirring constantly, and cook until thickened. Add margarine and beaten egg yolks. Fold in chicken and onion. Beat egg whites until stiff and fold into chicken mixture. Bake in 6 x 10-inch, greased baking dish at 375° for 40 minutes.

**We can get hot and bothered quicker over nothing, and cool off faster than any nation in the world.**

*—Will Rogers*

Ω

## SHREDDED SWISS CHEESE PIE

1 *cup milk*
4 *eggs*
½ *teaspoon salt*
½ *cup finely chopped, smoked beef*
1 *cup shredded Swiss cheese*

In mixing bowl, beat milk, eggs and salt and stir in beef and Swiss cheese. Pour into pie shell and bake at 350° for 30 to 40 minutes. Allow pie to stand 10 minutes before serving.

## BULLDOGGER STYLE GOULASH

*3 tablespoons margarine or butter*
*6 onions, chopped*
*2 pounds stew meat, cut into chunks*
*¼ cup paprika*
*1½ teaspoons salt*
*1 (8-ounce) container sour cream*
*4 cups buttered, cooked noodles*

In 5-quart Dutch oven over medium high heat, melt butter and cook onions until tender. Add stew meat, paprika and salt. Reduce heat to low, cover and simmer 1½ to 2 hours until hot. Serve over hot noodles. Makes 8 servings.

∩

## LARRUPIN' GOOD DUMPLINGS

*3 cups flour*
*3 teaspoons baking powder*
*3 teaspoons salt*
*6 teaspoons sugar*
*Milk*
*1 (8½-ounce) can chicken broth*

Mix all dry ingredients thoroughly, then add milk to make a stiff batter. Drop by teaspoon into broth of choice and cook for 20 minutes. Do not remove lid while cooking. (Carolyn Deffenbaugh)

**I never thought I'd live to see the day where women would get sunburned in the places they do now.**

—*Will Rogers*

## HOMEMADE PIONEER NOODLES

*1 cup sifted flour*
*¼ teaspoon salt*
*2 beaten eggs*
*1 tablespoon milk*
*Broth, chicken or beef*

Sift flour and salt together. Add eggs and stir. Add enough flour to make a thick mixture. Add milk and work into the rest of the mixture. Dump out onto floured board and knead until enough flour is worked in to make a soft dough and you are able to roll it out without sticking. After rolling, dust with flour and let set 30 minutes. Roll dough jelly-roll fashion. Cut into thin strips, shake out and let dry. Cook in hot chicken or beef broth. (Loistine Norfleet)

∩

## MACARONI AND TOMATOES

*2 tablespoons butter*
*1 small onion, diced*
*1 tablespoon minced green pepper*
*1 cup stewed tomatoes*
*½ teaspoon salt*
*2 cups cooked macaroni*
*¼ cup grated cheese*
*¼ teaspoon pepper*

Melt butter in skillet, add onion and green pepper and cook until tender. Add tomatoes, salt and simmer gently. Place cooked macaroni in a greased casserole dish. Pour sauce over it and sprinkle grated cheese on top. Bake at 375° for 30 minutes.

**When I growed up down in Indian Territory, we figured you could just talk to a feller and tell how smart he was. Sometimes you could just look at him.**

—Will Rogers

**[121]**

## BASIC WHITE SAUCE

*4 tablespoons butter or margarine, melted*
*4 tablespoons flour*
*½ teaspoon salt*
*¼ teaspoon pepper*
*2 cups milk*

Into melted butter, stir in flour, salt and pepper and cook 3 minutes on low heat, stirring well. Blend in milk and stir constantly until mixture thickens and bubbles.

## NEW MEXICO STYLE MACARONI

*3 cups uncooked macaroni shells*
*1 (4-ounce) can chopped green chilies, drained*
*1 (2-ounce) jar diced pimientos, drained*
*1 cup half-and-half cream*
*½ cup shredded cheddar cheese*
*½ cup sliced cheese*
*½ cup sliced green olives*
*½ teaspoon salt*

Cook macaroni according to package directions and drain. Stir in green chilies, pimientos, half-and-half cream, cheddar cheese, olives and salt. Cook over low heat, stirring occasionally, until cheese is melted and sauce is hot. Makes 6 servings.

## BROCCOLI CHEESE CASSEROLE

1 (10-ounce) box frozen, chopped broccoli
½ cup butter
½ cup chopped onion
1 cup instant rice
1 (10¾-ounce) can cream of chicken soup
½ cup water
½ milk
1 cup cubed Velveeta cheese

Cook broccoli and drain well. Add remaining ingredients. Bake at 350° for 30 to 40 minutes. (Cindy Baughman)

∩

## GARDEN RANCH LINGUINI

8 ounces linguini, cooked, drained
2 cups cooked mixed vegetables
2 cups cubed, cooked chicken
1 cup Ranch dressing
1 tablespoon grated Parmesan cheese

Combine all ingredients in large pan. Toss well. Heat through. Sprinkle with Parmesan cheese. (Cindy Baughman)

I was picked out of all the Hollywood actors to appear in *A Texas Steer*. The other actors all have morality clauses in their contracts and are afraid to act like a congressman.
—*Will Rogers*

## CHUCK WAGON GOULASH

1 pound ground beef
1 onion, chopped
2 cups chopped tomatoes
1 cup uncooked macaroni
1 cup water
1 teaspoon salt
Dash pepper
Dash basil
Dash garlic powder
Dash oregano

Brown ground beef and onion in skillet and drain. Add tomatoes, macaroni, water, salt and the rest of the seasonings. Mix and cook until macaroni is done.

∩

## MAC-A-RONI DINNER

1 (8-ounce) package elbow macaroni
2 tablespoons minced onion
½ teaspoon salt
¼ teaspoon garlic powder
1 tablespoon butter, melted
5 frankfurters
1 cup cottage cheese
1 cup shredded cheddar cheese

**Borrowing is the American way. How else did the national debt get so big?**

—Will Rogers

Cook macaroni according to package directions and drain. In small skillet sauté onion, salt and garlic powder in butter until onions are tender. Cut frankfurters into 1-inch pieces. Combine macaroni, onion mixture, frankfurters, cottage cheese and sour cream in casserole dish. Toss lightly until well mixed. Spread cheddar cheese on top. Bake at 350° for 30 minutes.

## GARLIC CHEESE CASSEROLE

*3 cups water*
*1 cup grits*
*1 teaspoon salt*
*1 roll garlic cheese*
*¾ stick butter*
*2 eggs, beaten*
*Hot sauce*

Bring water and salt to a boil in large saucepan. Reduce heat to medium and stir in grits and cook, stirring constantly, until they become thick. Remove from heat. Chop cheese and butter into chunks and add grits, stir until they are melted and mixed well with grits. Stir in beaten eggs and hot sauce, mix well and pour into greased, casserole dish. Cover and bake at 350° about 1 hour.

**Politics ain't worrying this country one-tenth as much as a parking space.**
   —*Will Rogers*

Ω

## AUNT BESSIE'S 1920'S MACARONI AND CHEESE

*¾ cup macaroni*
*½ tablespoon salt*
*2 quarts water*
*1 cup grated cheese*
*1 tablespoon butter*
*2 cups dry, buttered breadcrumbs*

Cook macaroni in rapidly boiling, salted water until tender. Add cheese and butter and mix well. Cover with breadcrumbs. Bake at 350° for 25 minutes. Makes 6 servings.

## ROPER'S MACARONI DINNER

*1 (6-ounce) package macaroni*
*1 cup chopped celery*
*½ cup chopped onions*
*2½ cups chopped tomatoes*
*½ cup chopped green pepper*
*2½ teaspoons salt*
*¼ teaspoon pepper*
*2 cups cubed ham*
*2 tablespoons chopped parsley*
*1 cup grated American cheese, divided*

Cook macaroni in boiling, salted water, until tender. Rinse in cold water. Drain and set aside. Sauté celery, onions, tomatoes, green pepper and seasonings together until tender. Combine macaroni, vegetables, ham, parsley and ¾ cup grated cheese. Pour into greased, 2-quart casserole dish. Bake at 350° for 1 hour. Top with remaining grated cheese during last 5 minutes of baking.

Ω

## SAUSAGE PINEAPPLE SURPRISE

*1 pound pork sausage*
*1 (8¼-ounce) can sliced pineapple, drained*
*1 egg, well beaten*
*1 cup corn flake crumbs*
*2 tablespoons oil*

Shape sausage into 8 thin patties. Pat pineapple slices dry, place 1 slice on each of 4 sausage patties and top with another sausage patty. Seal edges and center to look like doughnuts. Dip patties in egg and roll each in corn flake crumbs. Slowly cook in hot oil until done, turning twice. Makes 4 servings.

## QUICK HAM AND POTATOES AU GRATIN

4 potatoes, halved
1½ cups cooked cubed ham
1 (10¾-ounce) can condensed
    cheddar cheese soup
½ cup sour cream
½ cup milk
1 cup frozen mixed vegetables, thawed

Heat oven to 350°. Spray 2-quart casserole dish with nonstick cooking spray. In large bowl, combine potatoes and ham. In medium saucepan, combine soup, sour cream, milk and vegetables and mix well. Cook over medium heat until thoroughly heated, stirring frequently. Add to potato mixture and mix well. Spoon into casserole dish and bake for 1¾ to 2 hours, stirring once. Makes 4 servings.

Brigham Young originated mass production, but Henry Ford was the guy that improved on it.

—Will Rogers

Ω

## AFTER WORK PORK CHOP DINNER

2 to 3 pork chops
1 tablespoon oil
Salt
Pepper
1 (1-pound) package frozen pasta
    with vegetables
¼ cup water
Parmesan cheese

In large skillet, brown pork chops in oil and season with salt and pepper. Add pasta and vegetable mixture and water. Reduce heat to medium, cover and cook, stirring occasionally for 10 to 12 minutes or until pork chops are no longer pink in center and pasta and vegetables are tender. Sprinkle with Parmesan cheese. Makes 2 to 3 servings.

[127]

## RANCH COMPANY CASSEROLE

*6 pork chops*
*6 potatoes, cooked, cubed*
*2 (10¾-ounce) cans green beans, drained*
*1½ cups milk*
*4 tablespoons flour*
*Butter*

Brown pork chops. Place layer of potatoes, green beans and then pork chops. Top with another layer of the same. Combine the milk and flour. Pour over meat and vegetables. Dot with butter. May garnish with onion rings or chopped onion if desired. Bake at 350° for 45 minutes or until chops are tender. (Donna McSpadden)

Ω

## BIG RED CHILE ENCHILADAS

*Oil*
*1 (15-ounce) can red chile enchilada*
   *sauce, mild or hot*
*½ onion, finely chopped*
*3 cups grated longhorn or colby cheese*
*12 corn tortillas*
*4 eggs*

Fry each tortilla in hot oil, about 10 seconds and drain excess oil between paper towels. Heat sauce in pan large enough to dip tortillas. Dip one at a time and place on serving plate. Layer chopped onion and cheese until the stack is three high. Keep in a warm oven until all enchiladas are made. Top each with fried egg and serve immediately. Shred some lettuce to serve on the side. Pinto beans (frijoles) are also a good side dish. Makes 4 servings.

This type of enchilada is very typical of the New Mexico Southwest. Keep red sauce on hand for a really quick supper. Preparation time: 20 minutes.

**You go to the doctor and say, 'Doctor, I've got something wrong with my right eye.' He'll say, 'I'm sorry, I'm a left eye doctor.'**

—*Will Rogers*

# GREEN CHILE ENCHILADAS

1 (10¾-ounce) can cream of mushroom soup

½ soup can milk

1 (4-ounce) can chopped, green chile,
   hot or mild

8 to 12 corn tortillas

1 small onion, finely chopped

1 (6-ounce) package shredded, Monterey Jack
   cheese or colby

Mix soup, milk and green chile in small saucepan and heat until bubbly. In a small casserole dish, place a tortilla, top with sauce, sprinkle with onion and cheese. Continue stacking remaining tortillas, alternating with sauce until you run out of sauce. Bake at 325° for about 20 minutes until heated through and cheese is melted. Serve with salad and pinto beans. Makes 3 to 4 servings. This recipe can be made fat free. For a bigger crowd, double the recipe and use a larger casserole dish, tearing some tortillas to fill up the spaces.

Alice Ririe grew up in New Mexico where this dish was common and the ingredients were always on hand for a quick supper. For variation, use cream of chicken soup, or add sour cream to the sauce or as a garnish.

> **About all I do when I go back to Oklahoma is just shake hands and eat.**
>
> —*Will Rogers*

## CHILE RELLENOS CASSEROLE

*1 tablespoon margarine or butter*
*1 cup chopped onions*
*2 (4½-ounce) can, chopped green chilies,
    drained*
*1½ cups shredded cheddar cheese*
*1½ cups shredded Monterey Jack cheese*
*3 eggs*
*¾ cup sour cream*
*¼ teaspoon crushed, red pepper flakes*
*1 cup chopped, seeded tomatoes*

Melt margarine in skillet over medium-high heat. Add onions and stir until crisp-tender. Add green chilies. Spoon chile mixture evenly into greased pan. Sprinkle with cheese. In small bowl, beat eggs slightly, then add sour cream and red pepper flakes. Spoon egg mixture evenly over cheeses. Sprinkle with tomatoes. Bake at 350° for 35 to 45 minutes. Makes 6 servings

Ω

## ROBBIN'S BAKED CHILES RELLENOS
### Will Rogers Memorial, Jan Robbins

*8 fresh or canned long green chile peppers,
    peeled, split and seeded*
*2 cups grated, Monterey Jack cheese, divided*
*2 eggs*
*1 cup milk*
*Salt*
*Pepper*

Place open chiles flat. Place ½ of cheese on chile. Roll up each chile and place seam side down in greased 9 x 5 x 3-inch loaf pan. Beat eggs, milk, salt and pepper. Pour egg mixture over chiles and sprinkle with remaining cheese. Bake at 375° for 35-40 minutes or until puffed, brown and firm.

## INDIAN TACOS

1 cup flour
2 teaspoons baking powder
2 tablespoons sugar
1 teaspoon salt
1 tablespoon shortening
¾ cup warm milk
Flour
Oil for frying
Browned ground meat
Lettuce
Grated cheese
Chopped tomatoes
Chopped onion
Salsa

**Will Rogers could see humor in everything. "Everything is funny as long as it is happening to somebody else."**

In large bowl, stir together flour, baking powder, sugar and salt. Cut in shortening. With fork, gradually stir in enough milk to form a soft dough. Put on lightly floured board and knead until smooth. Roll out until ¼-inch thick. Cut into squares, pat to size of saucer and cut short slit in center of each. Heat oil in electric skillet to 350°, fry tortilla turning once, until puffed and golden. Top with any or all of the browned ground meat, lettuce, cheese, tomatoes, onion and salsa sauce.

## DENNY'S CHIMACHUNGAS

*2 cups cooked, shredded beef*
*1 onion, minced*
*½ cup chopped green pepper*
*1 clove garlic, minced*
*2 tablespoons oil*
*⅓ cup red chili sauce*
*1 cup refried beans*
*1 cup shredded Monterey Jack cheese*
*8 to 12 flour tortillas*
*Oil for frying*

Brown beef, onion, green pepper and garlic in oil. Drain, stir in chili sauce and simmer 1 minute. Stir in beans and cheese and remove from heat. Heat tortillas, fill with beef mixture. Fold in ends, roll up and deep fry. top with guacamole, cheese, onions and prepared salsa.

**Once a man holds public office he is absolutely no good for honest work.**

—Will Rogers

∩

## BULL RIDER'S TAMALE PIE

*2 cups chili con carne*
*7 tamales, cut into 1-inch pieces*
*2 cups broken corn chips*
*½ cup chopped onions*
*1 cup grated cheddar cheese*

Assemble chili con carne, tamales cut in 1-inch pieces, corn chips and chopped onions in baking dish. Top with cheese and bake at 350° for 30 minutes.

## CHIP BEEF ON TOAST

¼ pound chip beef
1 tablespoon butter
1 cup milk
1 ½ tablespoons flour
2 tablespoons cold water
Dash pepper
4 slices toast

Tear beef into pieces and put in a frying pan with butter. Stir and heat until butter is slightly browned. Pour milk over the beef. Put flour and cold water in a cup and stir until mixture is smooth. Stir milk and beef mixture and as you stir, pour in the flour and water mixture. Bring mixture to a full boil. Cook for 5 minutes longer. Add pepper and pour over toast. Makes 4 servings.

∩

## WHAT A CHEESEBURGER!

2 cups corned beef hash
½ cup sour cream
1 tablespoon pickle relish
1 teaspoon horseradish
Hamburger buns
2 tablespoons butter, melted
½ teaspoon dried mustard
4 fresh tomato slices
4 (1-ounce) slices cheddar cheese

Blend corned beef hash, sour cream, relish and horseradish and set aside. Place opened buns on baking sheet. Combine butter and mustard and brush on buns. Spread one side of each bun with hash mixture. Place a tomato slice on each and top with slice of cheddar cheese. Broil until cheese is bubbly.

I am not a member of any organized political party. I'm a Democrat. Actually, I keep saying I'm a Democrat, but I'm not. I just pretend to be one because they're funnier.

—Will Rogers

## STUFFED CRUST PIZZA CASSEROLE

*1 (10-ounce) can refrigerated pizza crust dough*
*1 (8-ounce) package string cheese*
*1 cup chopped onions*
*1 cup chopped, green bell pepper*
*1 tablespoon oil*
*1 (15-ounce) can southwestern chili beans*
*1 (14½-ounce) can diced, tomatoes, undrained*
*1 (6-ounce) can tomato paste*
*½ cup frozen corn*
*1 cup shredded cheddar cheese*

Heat oven to 425°. Grease 9 x 13-inch pan. Unroll pizza crust dough and place in greased pan. Starting at center, press out dough with hands over bottom and 1½-inches up sides. Place string cheese, end to end, around edge of dough, cutting to fit, if necessary. Fold edge of dough over cheese and pinch to seal under cheese. Bake at 425° for 10 minutes. Remove from oven. In large skillet cook onion and green pepper in oil 5 to 7 minutes, stirring occasionally. Add beans, tomatoes, tomato paste and corn; mix well. Bring to boil. Reduce oven to 375°. Spoon bean mixture evenly into partially baked crust. Sprinkle with cheddar cheese. Bake at 375° for 15 to 25 minutes or until crust is deep golden brown and cheese is melted. Let stand 3 minutes before serving. Makes 6 servings.

## STATE FAIR CORN DOG

*1 pound frankfurters*
*2 inches oil*
*1 cup cornmeal mix*
*½ cup milk*
*1 egg*
*1 teaspoon sugar*

Pat frankfurters dry with paper towels. Heat oil to 365°. Mix cornmeal mix, milk, egg and sugar. Dip frankfurters into batter, allowing excess batter to drip into bowl. Fry in hot oil, turning once, until golden brown. Drain on paper towels. Insert wooden skewer in end of each frankfurter.

Ω

## STAMPEDE SANDWICH

*2 loaves Italian bread, unsliced*
*1 (8-ounce) cream cheese, softened*
*4 ounces shredded cheddar cheese*
*¾ cup chopped green onions*
*¼ cup mayonnaise*
*1 tablespoon Worcestershire sauce*
*1 pound thinly sliced ham*
*1 pound thinly sliced roast beef*
*12 thinly sliced pickles*

Cut bread in half lengthwise. Hollow out top and bottom, leaving ½-inch shell. Combine cheeses, onions, mayonnaise and Worcestershire sauce and spread over bread. Layer ham and beef on both sides. Place pickles on bottom half. Gently press halves together. Wrap in plastic wrap. Refrigerate at least 2 hours. Cut in 1½-inch slices. Makes 12 to 14 servings. (Cindy Baughman)

**History has proven that there is nothing in the world so alike as two candidates. They look different until they get in, and then they all act the same.**

—*Will Rogers*

[135]

## COWBOY GUINEA GRINDER

*1 pound hamburger*
*1 pound hot sausage*
*1 onion, chopped*
*1 green pepper, chopped*
*1 (12-ounce) can tomato sauce*
*French bread*
*Mustard*
*Mozzarella cheese*

**Take your campaign contribution and send it to the Red Cross. Let the election be decided on its merit.**

*—Will Rogers*

Fry meats and drain. Add onion and green pepper and enough tomato sauce to hold mixture together. Split bread lengthwise and spread mustard on one side. Put mixture on bread and top with cheese and remaining half of bread. Wrap in foil. Bake at 350° for 30 minutes. (Cindy Baugham)

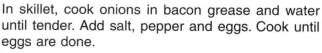

## WILD WEST ONION AND EGGS

*1½ cups chopped onions*
*2¼ tablespoons bacon grease*
*½ cup water*
*Salt*
*Pepper*
*4 eggs, beaten*

In skillet, cook onions in bacon grease and water until tender. Add salt, pepper and eggs. Cook until eggs are done.

## DOCTOR BULL BEEF SANDWICH

*2 pounds ground beef*
*½ cup chopped onion*
*1 teaspoon salt*
*½ teaspoon garlic powder*
*½ teaspoon pepper*
*1 loaf French bread, sliced*
*Butter*
*2 cups sour cream*
*2 tomatoes, diced*
*1 large green pepper, diced*
*3 cups shredded, cheddar cheese*

In skillet, brown beef and onion and drain. Add salt, garlic powder and pepper. Cut bread lengthwise in half, butter both halves and place on baking sheet. Remove meat mixture from heat and stir in sour cream. Spoon onto bread and sprinkle with tomatoes, green pepper and cheese. Bake at 350° for 20 minutes or longer for crispier bread. Makes 8 to 10 servings.

**A bunch of American tourists were hissed and stoned in France, but not until they had finished buying.**

*—Will Rogers*

## GRANNY'S BAKED BEANS

*2 (8-ounce) cans pork and beans*
*½ cup packed brown sugar*
*1 small onion, chopped*
*1 tablespoon Worcestershire sauce*
*3 tablespoons maple syrup*
*Bacon*

Combine beans, brown sugar, onion, Worcestershire sauce and syrup. Pour into casserole dish and top with bacon slices. Bake at 350° for ½ hour to 1 hour.

## BROCCOLI CHEDDAR BAKE

*1 (10¾-ounce) can cheddar cheese soup*
*¼ cup milk*
*4 cups cooked broccoli, cut up*
*1 (2.8-ounce) can French fried onions, divided*

In 1½-quart casserole dish, mix soup, milk, broccoli and ½ can fried onions. Bake at 350° for 25 minutes. Stir and sprinkle remaining fried onions over broccoli mixture. Bake 5 minutes more. Makes 6 servings. (Joann Russell)

Ω

**This old country boy is doin' pretty good and that's because he's still an old country boy.**

*—Will Rogers*

## SCALLOPED POTATOES

*1 quart sliced potatoes*
*1 pint tomatoes, chopped*
*3 green peppers, minced*
*1 small onion, chopped*
*Salt*
*Pepper*
*1 cup cream*
*Cracker crumbs*

Boil potatoes in salted water. Drain and place in baking dish with tomatoes, green peppers, onion and salt and pepper. Cover with cream, add a few cracker crumbs to top and bake at 350° until done. (Grayce Davis)

## FIESTA HASH BROWNS

1 (5½-ounce) package hash brown potatoes
   with onions, divided
1 (4-ounce) can chopped, green chilies, drained,
   divided
1 cup shredded Monterey Jack cheese, divided
3 tablespoons margarine or butter, divided

Cover potatoes with boiling water and let stand 5 minutes. Drain thoroughly. Layer half each of the potatoes, chilies and cheese in an ungreased 8 x 8 x 2-inch baking dish. Dot with half the margarine. Repeat with remaining ingredients. Cover and bake for 20 minutes at 350°. Uncover and bake until golden brown. (Judy Krause)

∩

## LISA'S HASH BROWNS

1 (2-pound) package frozen hash browns
1 cup sour cream
½ cup chopped onions
1 teaspoon salt
1 (10¾-ounce) can cream of celery soup
2 cups grated cheddar cheese
½ teaspoon pepper
¼ cup margarine, melted
2 cups crushed corn flakes

Mix all ingredients except margarine and corn flakes in 9 x 13-inch pan. Top with melted butter and corn flakes. Bake at 350° for 1 hour. (Lisa Higgins)

Every man has wanted to be a cowboy. Why play Wall Street and die young when you can play cowboy and never die?

—Will Rogers

[139]

## SWEET POTATO CASSEROLE

*3 cups cooked, mashed sweet potatoes*
*½ cup white sugar*
*2 eggs*
*¼ cup butter, melted*
*½ cup milk*
*1 teaspoon salt*
*Dash cinnamon*

**The truth can hurt you worse in an election that about anything than could happen to you.**

—*Will Rogers*

Mix all ingredients together. Pour into a 9 x 12-inch casserole dish. Make topping and add to casserole .

**Sweet Potato Topping:**

*½ cup packed brown sugar*
*¼ cup butter*
*½ cup flour*
*¼ cup chopped pecans*

Mix together brown sugar, butter and flour until crumbly. Distribute evenly over casserole. sprinkle chopped pecans over top. Bake at 350° about 30 minutes.

FROM THE RANCH,
HEN HOUSE
AND FISHING HOLE

[meat, poultry
and seafood]

**Will Rogers "On the Air"**

Will Rogers' early radio broadcasts were sponsored by E. J. Squibb Drug Company. Gulf Oil later sponsored his show. Once Gulf wanted Will to do a series of radio broadcasts for which he would be paid $60,000. Will was busy with other things and turned it down. Gulf Oil kept asking Will to do the show and he kept declining. Finally Betty said, "Will, why don't you do these radio shows and donate the proceeds to your favorite charities?" Will agreed and had Gulf send half to the Red Cross and the other half to the Salvation Army.

Will Rogers was on the first coast-to-coast radio broadcast in the United States. It had Paul Whiteman's Orchestra in New York, Al Jolson in New Orleans, Fred Stone in Chicago, and Will Rogers in Beverly Hills. The Dodge Victory Hour spent $67,000 for a forty-five station hookup to sell a $600 car.

Will Rogers had a problem with radio. It had no live audience, and required split second timing. Will was used to rambling on and saying whatever popped into his head. He solved this problem by bringing an alarm clock to the studio. When his time was up it rang. Will quickly wrapped things up (sometimes arguing with the alarm clock) and signed off. The alarm clock became a popular trademark for Will, much as his chewing gum had became in his live shows.

Will Rogers was a sports fan and often wrote of sporting events in his newspaper column. He loved for the underdog to prevail against overwhelming odds. Some events he especially liked was tiny Carr Creek High School

from the mountains of eastern Kentucky winning the Kentucky Basketball Championship Tourney; little Centre College defeating mighty Harvard in football; and Claremore, Oklahoma, native Andy Payne winning the across the country foot race from California to New York.

Will Rogers was the highest paid radio speaker of his time, earning five hundred dollars per minute of his fifteen minute broadcast, with broadcast executives begging him for more time.

**Will Rogers pecking out his daily newspaper column from the front seat of his car on Fox Studios lot.**

Will Rogers and Texas newsman Amon G. Carter.

(left) Will Rogers and news commentator Walter Winchell in New York about 1930.

Will Rogers with H. L. Mencken and Amon Carter (right), and unidentified man (left).

## SOUTHERN FRIED CHICKEN

*½ cup oil*
*1½ teaspoons salt*
*1 teaspoon pepper*
*1 (2½ to 3-pound) fryer chicken, cut-up*
*1 cup flour*

**A breakfast without a newspaper is like a horse without a saddle. We are just riding bareback if you got no news for breakfast. Take my ham away, take away my eggs, even my chili, but leave me my newspaper.**

—Will Rogers

Heat oil in skillet for frying. Salt and pepper chicken and roll in flour. Cook in oil and brown chicken on all sides. Turn heat on low and cover and simmer 20 minutes. Uncover and cook 5 minutes longer on high heat, turning frequently. Remove chicken and keep warm. Makes 4 to 6 servings.

### Can't Fail Chicken Gravy

*¼ cup chicken drippings*
*3 tablespoons flour*
*Salt*
*Pepper*
*2½ cups milk*

Remove chicken from skillet. Keep ¼ cup chicken drippings in skillet. Heat to medium, stir in flour, salt and pepper, cook until flour is golden and bubbly, at least 1½ minutes. If it gets dark, that's OK. Pour milk in skillet and keep stirring until thickened. Cook 1½ minutes more. Add more milk, if needed.

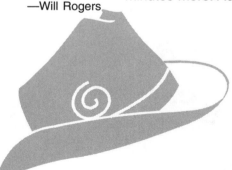

## PRETZEL FRIED CHICKEN

1 (3-pound) chicken, cut up
2 eggs, beaten
½ cup milk
3 cups finely chopped pretzels
Oil

Clean and dry the pieces of chicken with paper towel. Mix the eggs and milk. Place the finely crushed pretzels in a paper sack. Dip each piece of chicken in the egg/milk mixture; then place in the crushed prezels and shake until coated. Drop into 350° oil and fry until bolden brown. Place the fried chicken on large flat baking pan. Bake at 300° for 35 minutes.

> We will never have true civilization until we have learned to recognize the rights of others.
>
> —Will Rogers

∩

## HUSH-PUPPY FRIED CHICKEN

½ cup flour
½ cup yellow cornmeal
1 (3-pound) chicken, cut-up
½ teaspoon salt
¼ teaspoon pepper
1 cup buttermilk
1½ cup hush-puppy mix
Oil

Mix the flour and corn meal together in a paper sack. Place each piece of chicken in the sack and shake to coat. Mix the salt, pepper and buttermilk together. Place the hush-puppy mix in another paper sack. Dip each piece of chicken in the seasoned buttermilk and then drop it into the hush-puppy mix and shake to coat. Heat oil to 350°and fry chicken until a rich golden brown. Place in a flat baking dish and bake at 350° for 30 minutes.

# PAPER BAG BARBECUED CHICKEN

*2 teaspoons catsup*

*2 teaspoons white vinegar*

*2 teaspoons butter*

*2 teaspoons Worcestershire sauce*

*4 teaspoons water*

*2 teaspoons lemon juice*

*1 teaspoon mustard*

*1 teaspoon salt*

*1 teaspoon paprika*

*1 teaspoon chili powder*

*1 tablespoon sugar*

*1 (3-pound) chicken, cut-up*

**Common sense is not an issue in politics, it's an affliction.**

*—Will Rogers*

Heat oven to 500°. Grease a brown paper bag. Place all ingredients except chicken in saucepan and heat. Dip chicken pieces in sauce and place in a well-greased paper bag. (If any sauce is left, pour it in the bag with chicken.) Fold paper bag closed and place it in a roaster with tight cover. Bake at 500° for 15 minutes, then reduce heat to 350° and bake 1 hour and 20 minutes.

## DELICIOUSLY DIFFERENT BAKED CHICKEN

*8 slices white bread, divided*
*2 cups cooked, chopped chicken, divided*
*1 (10-ounce) package cut asparagus, cooked*
*1 cup grated cheddar cheese, divided*
*1 (10¾-ounce) can cream of chicken soup*
*½ cup milk*
*¼ cup chopped pimientos, drained*

Trim crust from bread and place 4 slices on the bottom of a square 8-inch baking dish. Layer alternately with half of the chicken, cooked asparagus and remaining chicken. Top with half the grated cheese. Combine chicken soup, milk and pimientos. Pour ½ of soup mixture over chicken. Cover with remaining 4 slices bread. Pour remaining soup mixture over bread. Sprinkle with remaining cheese. Bake at 325° for 40 minutes. Makes 4 servings.

Ω

## FINGER-LICKIN' CHICKEN

*3 pounds meaty chicken pieces*
*¾ cup honey*
*¾ cup buttermilk baking mix*
*2 teaspoons dried mustard*
*½ teaspoon paprika*
*Salt*
*Pepper*
*Vegetable oil*

Coat chicken with honey and set aside. Combine buttermilk baking mix, mustard, paprika, salt and pepper and dredge chicken in mixture. Heat oil to 375° in a 12-inch skillet over medium heat. Cook chicken in hot oil for about 5 minutes, turning as needed. Reduce heat to low and cook 10 minutes longer. Drain on paper towels. Makes 6 servings.

> **A lot of times you have to vote for somebody you don't want to just to keep somebody worse out. It seems like every election we get in worse men and the country just keeps right on going. Times have proven one thing and that is you can't ruin this country ever with politics.**
>
> —*Will Rogers*

## GEORGIA PEACH CHICKEN ROAST

1 (2 or 3-pound) chicken, cut-up
1 (14-ounce) can peach halves in heavy syrup, reserve syrup
2 tablespoons chopped onions
2 tablespoons soy sauce
½ cup butter
1 teaspoon Accent
12 maraschino cherries

A press agent is not to see how much they can get in the papers about their clients, but how much they can prevent from gettin' in the papers.

—Will Rogers

Place pieces of chicken in roasting pan without letting them overlap. In saucepan, heat the syrup from the peaches to just below boiling point. Add chopped onions, soy sauce, butter and Accent. Baste each piece of chicken generously with this mixture. Place in oven at 375° for 1½ hours, basting frequently. When the chicken is golden brown and tender, place each peach half up around the chicken. Place cherry in center of each peach. Return to the oven for an additional 8 minutes or until peaches are warm.

## STUFFED CHICKEN BAKE

1 (6 to 8-pound) chicken
Butter
Salt
Pepper
6 cups breadcrumbs
1 cup chopped apples
½ cup chopped walnuts
1 onion, chopped
1 tablespoon poultry seasoning

Clean and dry chicken. Rub butter over chicken and salt and pepper. Mix breadcrumbs, apples, walnuts, onions, poultry seasoning and stuff chicken. Cover with foil and bake at 350° for 3 hours. Remove foil and brown 10 to 40 minutes. (Francis Logan)

## CHICKEN PARMESAN

1 (8-ounce) can tomato sauce
½ tablespoon Italian seasoning
¼ tablespoon garlic salt
⅓ cup cracker crumbs
¼ cup grated Parmesan cheese
1 tablespoon dried parsley flakes
4 boneless, skinless, chicken breasts
1 egg, beaten
Mozzarella cheese, grated

Combine tomato sauce, Italian seasoning and garlic salt. Microwave on high 2 minutes and stir. Cook 5 minutes on medium. In dish combine cracker crumbs, Parmesan cheese and parsley. Dip chicken breasts in egg, then crumb mixture. Place in baking dish. Bake at 350° for 45 minutes. Pour sauce over chicken and top with mozzarella cheese. Bake at 350° for 15 minutes. (Cindy Baughman)

**There is an old legend that years ago there was a man elected to Washington who voted accordin' to his own conscience.**

*—Will Rogers*

∩

## BEST EVER CHICKEN

⅓ cup plain breadcrumbs
1 (4-ounce) package buttermilk ranch salad dressing mix
⅓ cup sour cream
4 boneless, skinless chicken breasts, halved

In pie pan, combine breadcrumbs and salad dressing and mix well. Pour sour cream in another pie pan. Dip chicken in sour cream and coat well. Roll coated chicken in breadcrumb mixture. Place chicken on sprayed cookie sheet. Bake for 30 to 35 minutes at 375°. Makes 4 servings. (Joann Russell)

## DIPPING CHICKEN FINGERS

*Cooking spray*
*¾ cup plain breadcrumbs*
*3 tablespoons Parmesan cheese*
*1 pound chicken tenderloins*
*2 eggs, beaten*
*1 cup barbecue sauce*

Spray cookie sheet with nonstick cooking spray. In small bowl, combine breadcrumbs and cheese and mix. Dip chicken tenders into beaten egg and roll in bread-crumbs, coating evenly. Place on cookie sheet. Bake at 375° for 30 minutes or until chicken is no longer pink and coating is crisp. Serve with barbecue sauce for dipping.

Ω

## CHICKEN CRUNCH

*4 (10¾-ounce) cans cream of mushroom soup*
*1 cup chicken broth*
*1 cup finely chopped onions*
*3 cups diced celery*
*8 cups chopped, cooked chicken*
*1 (13-ounce) can chow mein noodles, divided*
*2 cups salted cashew nuts*

Heat oven to 325°. Mix together mushroom soup, chicken broth, onions, celery and chicken. Arrange alternate layers of noodles and chicken mixture in shallow pan, but save some noodles for top. Sprinkle noodles and nuts over top. Bake for 35 minutes. Makes 20 servings.

## CRUSTY STUFFED CHICKEN BREASTS

½ cup mayonnaise

3 tablespoons mustard

1 stick butter or margarine, melted

8 boneless chicken breasts

1 (8-ounce) package herbed stuffing mix,
   crushed

Heat oven to 350°. Use 9 x 9 x 2-inch baking dish. Mix mayonnaise, mustard and butter. Dip chicken breasts in mixture and roll in stuffing. Place the breasts in baking dish. If there is stuffing left, stir it with the remaining butter mixture and sprinkle it around the breasts. Cover and bake at 350° for 1 hour, then remove cover and bake for an additional 30 minutes. Do not salt chicken.

∩

## CHICKEN FOLD-UPS

8 (6-ounce) boneless, skinless chicken breasts

1 cup flour

1 teaspoon salt

½ teaspoon pepper

8 tablespoons almond slivers

8 tablespoons seasoned breadcrumbs

1 tablespoon butter

8 thin ham slices

½ cup shortening

1 (6-ounce) can frozen orange juice, thawed

Preheat oven to 350°. Wash and roll chicken breasts in flour, salt and pepper. Sauté almonds and breadcrumbs in butter. Place one tablespoon on a ham slice and roll-up. Make cut in center of chicken and place ham in the center. Fold up breast and secure around ham with toothpick. Brown on all sides in shortening. Pour orange juice over breasts. Cover and bake at 350° for 40 minutes.

I don't make jokes. I just watch the government and report the facts and I have never found it necessary to exaggerate.

—*Will Rogers*

[153]

## CHICKEN BREASTS SUPREME

1 (4-ounce) package, chipped beef
4 boneless chicken breasts, halved
8 slices bacon
1 (8-ounce) container sour cream
1 (10¾-ounce) can cream of mushroom soup
1¼ cup water
Rice or noodles, optional

Heat oven to 275°. Grease baking dish and put in chipped beef. Wrap each chicken breast half in a slice of bacon. Place chicken on a bed of chipped beef. Combine sour cream, soup and water and pour the mixture over chicken. Bake 2 hours. Serve on rice or noodles, if desired. Makes 8 servings.

Ω

## CHICKEN CHINESE

4 boneless, skinless chicken breasts, halved
Salt
Pepper
½ cup flour
½ stick margarine, melted
2 tablespoons soy sauce
2 tablespoons pineapple juice
1 tablespoon chopped onions
½ teaspoon ground ginger
¼ teaspoon cardamon

Wash chicken breasts and coat with salt, pepper and flour. Place each piece of chicken on an individual square of aluminum foil. Mix all remaining ingrents and pour equal amounts over chicken pieces. Wrap foil tightly so package will not leak. Bake at 350° for 1½ hours. Makes 8 servings.

**I have found when newspapers knock a man a lot, there is sure to be a lot of good in him.**

—Will Rogers

## GLAZED CHICKEN BREASTS

½ cup apple butter
½ cup molasses
¾ teaspoon ground ginger
½ teaspoon pepper
½ teaspoon salt
4 boneless, skinless, chicken breasts

In bowl, stir together apple butter, molasses, ginger, pepper and salt. Add chicken and toss to coat. Cover and refrigerate for 30 minutes. Line broiler pan with aluminum foil and set chicken in it. Broil 20 minutes, turning occasionally and brushing with marinade. Makes 4 servings.

Ω

## THAT'S A SPICEY CHICKEN
**Will Rogers Memorial, Patty VanPelt, Gift Shop**

4 boneless, skinless chicken breasts, cubed
6 green onions, chopped
1 box Spanish rice
1 (15-ounce) can Rotel tomatoes and green chilis
1 (6-ounce) can chopped black olives, drained
1 (15-ounce) can whole kernel corn, drained
1 cup sour cream
Pepper to taste

Brown chicken until very dark, adding pepper as you go. Stir in green onions right before the chicken is done. Remove from skillet and set aside. In same skillet, fix rice according to package directions using Rotel instead of tomatoes. When rice is ready to simmer, add chicken back to skillet and stir in olives and corn. Cover and simmer 15 minutes. Add sour cream and stir until heated. Makes 4 to 6 servings.

> Put the President on a farm with the understandin' that he has to make a livin' on it, the farmers will get relief next year.
>
> —Will Rogers

## TEXAS SKIP BAKED CHICKEN

*2 tablespoons oil*
*6 boneless, skinless chicken breasts, halved*
*½ cup milk*
*1 (10¾-ounce) can cream of mushroom soup*
*1 tablespoon fresh parsley*
*Salt*
*Pepper*

In skillet heat oil and brown chicken; then drain. Place chicken in baking dish. Mix milk, soup and parsley and pour into same skillet chicken was browned in. Heat to a boil and pour over chicken. Cover and bake at 375° for 15 minutes. Uncover and bake 30 minutes. Makes 6 servings.

Ω

## WILL ROGERS' CHICKEN LIVERS AND MUSHROOMS

*1 cup fresh mushrooms, sliced*
*6 tablespoons butter, divided*
*12 chicken livers, parboiled*
*Salt*
*Pepper*
*Toast*

Sauté mushrooms in 3 tablespoons butter. Parboil chicken livers and sauté them in remaining butter with sautéed mushrooms. Season with salt and pepper and serve on toast.

## DELICIOUSLY MOIST, BAKED TURKEY

1 (19 to 20-pound) turkey
1½ cup butter
Salt
1 cup water

Clean and dry turkey and put in roasting pan. Rub butter over turkey and salt to season. Pour hot water in roasting pan. Put heavy foil over turkey to seal it completely. Bake at 350° for 4 hours, take tin foil off and spoon juice over turkey. Recover and bake until golden brown. Do not take tinfoil off while cooking.

**Turkey Gravy:**

½ cup flour
¼ cup milk
4 tablespoons butter, melted
½ teaspoon pepper
1 teaspoon salt
2 cups turkey broth

**All I know is what I read in the newspapers. I don't make up my little jokes, I just tell what happens and that does it.**

—*Will Rogers*

Remove turkey from roasting pan. Mix flour and milk until smooth. Add butter, pepper and salt to turkey broth and bring to a boil. Pour flour and milk mixture into the broth and cook on low heat, stirring until thick.

## MISSOURI SMOTHERED PHEASANT

*12 pheasant halves*
*⅓ cup oil*
*2 tablespoons butter*
*2 (10¾-ounce) cans cream of mushroom soup*
*2 (10¾-ounce) cans cream of celery soup*
*1 (10-ounce) can onion soup*
*3 (10-ounce) soup cans of water*
*Salt*
*Pepper*
*Wild rice*

> A politician's thoughts are naturally on his next term, more than on his country.
> —Will Rogers

In heavy skillet brown pheasant halves in mixture of cooking oil and butter until both sides are golden. Arrange the halves with meat side down in a roaster. Mix soups and water and pour over the halves. Cover and bake at 350° for approximately 1 hour. Reduce heat to 300° and cook ½ hour longer or until tender. Serve with wild rice. Makes 12 servings. (Janet Habick)

## OLD SETTLER'S BAKED QUAIL

*½ cup butter*
*2 tablespoons oil*
*1 quail*
*½ cup flour*
*Salt*
*Pepper*
*1 cup or more light cream*

Heat butter and oil in skillet. Dredge quail with flour, salt and pepper and brown on all sides in hot oil. Push quail to side of skillet and pour off excess oil. Loosen particles on skillet and add light cream. Stir well with pan drippings, cover quail and simmer over gentle heat (do not boil) until tender. Add more cream as needed. (Claude Reasoner).

## CHICKEN FRIED STEAK
**Will Rogers Memorial, Carol L. Low**

*1 egg, beaten*
*¼ cup milk*
*Salt*
*Pepper*
*1 cup flour*
*1 (1½-pound) round steak, tenderized*
*Oil*

Mix egg, salt, pepper and milk. Put flour in separate shallow pan. Cut round steak in serving pieces. Dip each piece of steak in flour, cover both sides and then dip in egg mixture. Dip again in flour, place in skillet with hot oil and brown on both sides. Lower heat to simmer until done. Pour gravy over steak.

**You can get a road anywhere you want to out of the government, but you can't get a sandwich.**

—*Will Rogers*

**Dripping Gravy:**

*Oil*
*¼ cup flour*
*Salt*
*Pepper*
*Milk*

Remove steak from pan. Scrape pan with spatula to loosen cooked bits. Pour into measuring cup if needed and add oil to make ¼ cup. Return drippings to skillet and add ¼ cup flour, salt and pepper and cook on medium heat. Stir until flour bubbles. Add milk and stir until thick and smooth. Pour over meat.

## WILL'S CHICKEN FRIED STEAK
### Will Rogers Memorial Gift Shop, Juna Phillips

*4 serving pieces round steak, tenderized*
*Garlic clove*
*Salt*
*Pepper*
*1 to 2 eggs*
*½ cup milk*
*Flour*
*Oil*

Rub steak lightly with fresh garlic clove and season with salt and pepper. Dip steak in beaten egg, then in flour. Fry in moderately hot oil until brown.

∩

## COUNTRY FRIED STEAK

*1 (1-pound) round steak, tenderized*
*½ cup flour*
*1½ teaspoons salt*
*½ teaspoon pepper*
*1 egg, beaten*
*Oil*
*¼ cup water*
*1 medium onion, sliced thinly*
*Milk*

Cut steak into 4 pieces. Coat with flour, salt and pepper. Dip steak in egg, then return to seasoned flour. Heat oil in skillet over medium heat and brown steak on both sides. Add water and onion, cover and simmer 1 hour. Remove steak from skillet and add remaining seasoned flour mix. Simmer 3 minutes, stirring frequently. Add milk and stir until thick. Serve on steak. Makes 4 servings.

# MOM'S BEEF ROAST

¼ cup oil
1 stick margarine
Salt
Pepper
1 cup flour
1 (2 to 3-pound) beef roast
1½ cups hot water

In skillet, heat oil and butter. Salt, pepper and flour roast. Put in skillet and brown on all sides, about 30 minutes on low heat. In heavy pan, put roast and add hot water, cover and bring to a boil. Turn heat on low and cook 2 to 3 hours. Add more water when needed. (Marie Elifritz)

**A tax paid on the day you buy is not as tough as askin' you for it the next year when you are broke.**

—Will Rogers

Ω

# BLACK COFFEE ROAST BEEF

1 (3½-to-4-pound) roast
4 cloves garlic, halved
2 tablespoons cooking oil
1 yellow onion, quartered
1 tablespoon tomato paste
2 cups medium black coffee
2 cups water
1 tablespoon butter
½ cup red wine

Preheat oven to 450°. Using a sharp knife, make very small cuts in the roast and insert the garlic halves. Heat the oil in a heavy roasting pan and brown the roast on all sides. Add the onion, tomato paste, coffee and water to pan and roast for 30 minutes. Reduce the heat to 375° and cook for 1½ hours or until roast is done to taste. Remove the roast, let cool slightly and then slice. Stir the butter and wine into the pan juices and serve with the sliced roast. Makes 8 to 10 servings.

## DELICIOUS ROAST 'N GRAVY

*Salt*
*Pepper*
*½ cup flour*
*1 (3-pound) roast beef*
*¼ cup oil*
*2 tablespoons margarine*
*1 soup can milk*
*2 (10¾-ounce) cans cream of mushroom soup*

> **War strikes me as bein' the only game in the world where there is absolutely no winner—everybody loses.**
>
> —*Will Rogers*

Salt, pepper and flour roast on all sides. Brown roast in oil and margarine on low heat 10 minutes on each side. Put roast in baking dish. Mix milk and cream of mushroom soup and pour in skillet where roast was browned. Heat to boiling stage. Pour over roast. Cover and bake at 350° for 3 to 3½ hours.

Ω

## OKLAHOMA PEPPER STEAK

*1 (1-pound) round steak, tenderized*
*Oil*
*1 clove garlic, halved*
*2 tablespoons chopped onions*
*½ cup chopped celery*
*2 green peppers, sliced*
*1 beef bouillon cube, dissolved*
*1½ cups water, divided*
*2 tablespoons flour*
*1 teaspoon soy sauce*

Cut round steak in thin, ½-inch long slices. Brown in oil and garlic and remove garlic halves. Add onion, celery, peppers and bouillon cube dissolved in 1 cup water and let simmer for 20 minutes. Make a thickening of flour, ½ cup water and soy sauce. Add to the mixture and cook until thick. Pour over rice.

FROM THE RANCH, HEN HOUSE AND FISHING HOLE

## RUSTLER'S PEPPER STEAK

*1½ pounds round steak*
*Oil*
*½ cup catsup*
*1½ tablespoons flour*
*2 beef bouillon cubes, dissolved*
*2 tablespoons soy sauce*
*1½ cups water*
*Salt*
*Pepper*
*1 medium onion, sliced*
*1 (4-ounce) can mushrooms, drained*
*1 cup sliced green peppers*
*Oil*
*Steamed rice*

Cut steak in serving-size strips. Brown lightly in hot skillet in small amount of oil. Remove meat and add mixture of catsup, flour, bouillon, soy sauce and water to skillet. Simmer for 5 minutes. Return meat to skillet, cover and cook over gentle heat until steak is tender, about 1½ hours. Add salt and pepper to taste, onion slices, mushrooms and green peppers. Cover and steam until vegetables are just tender. Serve with steamed rice. Makes 4 to 6 servings.

You can't say civilization don't advance. In every war they kill you in a new way.

—*Will Rogers*

## BUNKHOUSE STEAK

⅓ cup honey
⅓ cup lime juice
2 tablespoons vegetable oil
2 tablespoons prepared mustard
2 cloves garlic, minced
1 teaspoon grated lime peel
½ teaspoon salt
½ teaspoon pepper
2 pounds top round steak

**You know an awful lot of folks don't know much about gravy. Ham gravy is just about the last word in gravys.**

*—Will Rogers*

Whisk together all ingredients except steak. Score steak across top and place in a shallow baking pan. Pour marinade over steak and turn to coat all sides. Refrigerate 6 to 8 hours, turning occasionally. Broil 6 inches from heat. Cook to desired doneness. Slice thinly on the diagonal. Makes 6 servings.

∩

## YANKEE BEEF STEAK

4 (6-ounce) top loin beef or New York strip steaks
2 tablespoons minced rosemary
2 cloves garlic, minced
1 tablespoon virgin olive oil
1 teaspoon grated lemon peel
1 teaspoon ground black pepper
½ teaspoon salt

Score steaks in diamond pattern on both sides. Combine rosemary, garlic, oil, lemon peel, pepper and salt in small bowl and rub mixture onto surface of meat. Cover and refrigerate 30 minutes. Grill steaks over medium hot fire for 4 minutes per side until desired doneness.

## TENDERLOIN OF BEEF WITH LOBSTER

1 (3 to 4-pound) tenderloin of beef
1 cup soy sauce, divided
2 tablespoons fresh ground ginger
1 onion, sliced thinly
¾ cup sherry wine, divided
3 lobster tails
4 tablespoons butter

Heat oven to 450°. Rub beef with ½ cup of soy sauce and ginger. Place on onion slices and cook for 25 minutes. Baste with half the sherry. Split lobster tails, loosen meat and rub with soy sauce. Bake at 350° for 10 minutes. Remove meat from shell. Split tenderloin ¾ deep and stuff lobster into cavity. Place under broiler and baste with remaining sherry and soy mixture. Leave under broiler only to heat. Sprinkle with chopped parsley and melted butter. Slice and serve with juices.

**It's up to the voter to believe one man's promise or another man's alibis.**

—*Will Rogers*

∩

## SWISS STEAK MY-WAY

1 ½ pounds round steak
¼ cup flour
1 teaspoon salt
½ teaspoon pepper
2 tablespoons shortening
2 cups canned tomatoes, chopped
3 whole cloves
2 slices onion
1 bay leaf
1 cup boiling water

Cut round steak in 1-inch thick pieces. Mix flour, salt and pepper and pound into both sides of steak. Brown on both sides in shortening. Pour tomatoes, whole cloves, onion, bay leaf and hot water in skillet. Let simmer on top of stove until tender.

[165]

# BAKED BEEF BRISKET

*1 (3 to 4–pound) beef brisket*
*Salt*
*Pepper*
*2 bay leaves*
*3½ ounces liquid smoke*
*6 tablespoons water*

**Radio is a tough thing for a comedian. That little microphone is not going to laugh.**
—*Will Rogers*

Wipe brisket of beef with a damp cloth. Sprinkle salt, pepper and bay leaves over brisket. Mix liquid smoke and water together. Marinate the brisket in liquid mixture overnight. Preheat oven to 250°. Remove brisket from marinade and wrap in heavy-duty aluminum foil. Place fat side up in a shallow baking pan. Bake for 6 hours. Serve with Horseradish sauce.

**Horseradish Sauce:**

*1 cup whipping cream*
*½ cup salad dressing*
*3 tablespoons mustard*
*1 tablespoon horseradish*
*1 teaspoon lemon juice*
*1 teaspoon Worcestershire sauce*
*½ teaspoon seasoned salt*
*Salt*
*Pepper*

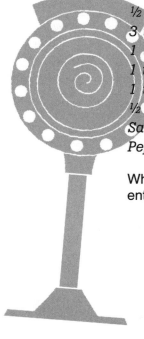

Whip cream in large bowl. Fold in remaining ingredients and chill.

## COWPUNCHER JOES

*1 pound ground beef*
*1 onion, chopped*
*1 (10¾-ounce) can condensed chicken gumbo soup*
*½ cup catsup*
*2 tablespoons vinegar*
*2 teaspoons mustard*
*½ teaspoon salt*

Brown ground beef and onion. Add remaining ingredients. Cook 25 minutes on low heat. Makes 4 to 6 servings.

∩

## ROUTE 66 BURGERS

*1½ pounds ground beef*
*1 package taco seasoning*
*¼ cup catsup*
*¼ teaspoon garlic salt*
*1 small onion, chopped*
*Monterey Jack cheese slices*
*Salsa*

In medium bowl, combine ground beef, taco seasoning, catsup, garlic, salt and onion and mix well. Shape into patties. Grill or broil burgers 10 to 15 minutes, turning halfway through cooking time and top with slices of cheese. Return to grill or broiler until cheese melts. Top with salsa. Makes 6 to 8 servings.

**All I know is what I read in the newspaper.**
—*Will Rogers*

## BUFFALO-STYLE BURGERS

*1 pound ground beef*
*½ cup sour cream*
*¼ cup dry breadcrumbs*
*1 (1½-ounce) package onion soup mix*

Mix all ingredients. Shape mixture into 4 patties. Broil 3 inches from heat until desired doneness. (Cindy Lowell)

∩

## SALISBURY STEAK

**I joked about every prominent man of my time, but I never met a man I didn't like.**

—*Will Rogers*

*1 pound ground beef*
*¾ cup finely chopped carrots*
*¾ cup finely chopped onions*
*Salt*
*Pepper*
*½ cup flour*
*2 tablespoons oil*
*2 tablespoons flour*
*¾ cup milk*
*1 (10¾-ounce) can cream of mushroom soup*

Mix ground beef, carrots and onions by hand. Add salt, pepper and flour and mix well. Make patties with meat mixture and brown well on both sides in skillet using oil. Place browned patties in baking dish. With drippings from patties, add 2 tablespoons flour to make gravy and add milk as needed. To gravy, add 1 can cream of mushroom soup. Cover patties with gravy. Cover and bake at 350° for 45 minutes to 1 hour.

## OLD-FASHIONED MEAT LOAF

1 ½ pounds ground beef
¼ cup chopped onions
1 egg, beaten
¾ cup milk
¾ cup uncooked oats
1 ½ teaspoons salt
¼ teaspoon pepper
¾ cup catsup
2 tablespoons brown sugar
1 tablespoon mustard

In bowl, mix ground beef, onion, egg, milk, oats, salt and pepper. Pack firmly into greased, loaf pan. Mix catsup, brown sugar and mustard and pour over meat loaf. Bake at 350° for 1 hour.

∩

## BRANDING IRON MEAT LOAF

1 ½ pound ground beef
¾ cup uncooked oatmeal
½ cup chopped onions
1 egg, beaten
1 ½ teaspoon salt
¼ teaspoon pepper
1 cup tomato juice
½ cup cream
Catsup

Mix all ingredients and pack firmly into greased loaf pan. Bake at 350° for 1 hour. Pour catsup on top and bake for 20 minutes more.

Congress—they are the professional joke makers. I could study all my life and not think up half the amount of funny things they can think of in one session of congress.

—Will Rogers

[169]

## BARBECUE MEAT LOAF

*1 pound ground beef*
*½ pound ground pork*
*½ cup breadcrumbs*
*¼ cup finely chopped onions*
*¼ cup parsley, snipped*
*2 eggs, beaten*
*1 cup barbecue sauce, divided*
*1 teaspoon dried mustard*

In large bowl, combine all meats and mix well. Add breadcrumbs, onions, parsley, eggs and ½ cup barbecue sauce. Mix until well blended. Press firmly in ungreased loaf pan. Bake at 350° for 50 minutes. Remove meat loaf from oven. Mix ½ cup barbecue sauce and mustard. Spread over top of meat loaf. Bake an additional 30 minutes. Makes 6 servings.

## ∩
## WESTERN LAMB CHOPS

**Death knows no denomination: Death draws no color line. If you live right, death is a joke as far as fear is concerned.**

—*Will Rogers*

*4 (1-inch) lamb chops*
*½ teaspoon salt*
*1 (12-ounce) jar thick salsa, divided*
*1 large tomato, sliced*
*1 large avocado, sliced*

Preheat broiler. Place lamb chops on rack in broiling pan. Sprinkle salt over chops, then spread with about half of salsa. Place pan in broiler at closest position to source of hear; broil 4 minutes. Turn chops and spread with remaining salsa. Broil 8 minutes longer for medium to rare or until desired doneness. Serve chops with tomato and avocado slices.

## TANGY PORK CHOPS

2 large onions, cut into thick slices
3 tablespoons oil, divided
4 (¾-inch) pork loin chops
¾ teaspoon salt
2 tablespoons brown sugar
2 tablespoons cider vinegar

In skillet over medium heat, cook onions in 2 tablespoons of oil until tender and set aside. Add pork chops and 1 tablespoon oil to skillet. Cook until pork is browned on both sides. In saucepan stir in salt, brown sugar and vinegar and heat to a boil, stirring until brown sugar dissolves. Pour over pork chops and cook 5 minutes.

Ω

## HOMESTEAD PORK CHOPS

6 pork chops
Oil
5 potatoes, peeled and halved
6 green onions, sliced julienne
3 celery ribs, sliced julienne
1 green pepper, sliced julienne
1 (16-ounce) can chopped tomatoes
Salt and pepper

In skillet brown pork chops in oil and then move pork chops to a baking dish. Lay potatoes, green onions and celery on top of pork chops. Sliver green pepper over onions and add tomatoes, salt and pepper. Cover tightly and bake at 350° for 1½ hours.

**What constitutes a life well spent? Love and admiration from your fellow man is all anyone can ask.**

—*Will Rogers*

[171]

## MARINATED PORK KABOBS

½ cup cider vinegar
1 onion, grated
1 teaspoon paprika
½ teaspoon salt
½ teaspoon dried basil or marjoram
¼ teaspoon pepper
1 pound tenderloin, cut in 1-inch chunks
8 ounces cherry tomatoes
2 zucchini, cut in 1-inch chunks
1 green pepper, cut in 1-inch pieces
1 large onion, cut in 8 wedges

In medium bowl, mix vinegar, grated onion, spices and pepper. Add pork and turn to coat with marinade. Cover and refrigerate at least 4 hours or overnight, turning pork several times. Put pork and veggies on skewers and marinade. Grill, basting frequently with marinade. (Cindy Baughman)

Ω

## PORKY SURPRISE

4 cups cut-up, cooked pork
1 large onion, sliced
2 cups barbecue sauce

Cook and stir pork and onion in a 3-quart saucepan over medium heat until onion is tender and pork is brown on all sides, about 10 minutes. Stir in barbecue sauce. Simmer 10 minutes. Serve over rice, spaghetti or noodles. (Joann Russell)

## PORK FAJITAS

1 pound pork tenderloin or loin
¼ cup Italian dressing
2 teaspoons oil
½ medium onion, sliced
1 cup sliced, green pepper
½ teaspoon garlic powder
2 tablespoons lemon juice
4 (8-inch) flour tortillas, warmed

Cut pork into thin strips. In heavy plastic bag, combine pork strips and dressing. Refrigerate several hours. Drain off liquid. Heat oil in nonstick skillet over medium high heat; stir-fry pork and onions for 5 minutes. Stir in green pepper and cook 5 minutes. Add garlic powder and lemon juice and toss to coat. Serve in warm tortillas. Makes 4 servings.

∩

## PINEAPPLE SPARERIBS

3 pounds spareribs
¾ cup packed brown sugar
½ cup pineapple juice
½ cup prepared mustard

Place ribs in baking dish. Combine all remaining ingredients and pour over ribs. Bake covered, basting occasionally, at 350° for 45 minutes. Uncover and bake 35 minutes.

**The Platform will always be the same, promise everythin', deliver nothin'. Can you imagine a man in public office that everybody knew where he stood? We wouldn't call him a statesman, we would call him a curiosity.**

—Will Rogers

## LICKIN GOOD SPARERIBS

*3 pounds pork spareribs*
*Salt*
*Pepper*
*1 tablespoon sugar*
*1 cup chili sauce*
*½ cup honey*
*¼ cup minced onions*
*1 tablespoon Worcestershire sauce*
*1 teaspoon mustard*

Sprinkle spareribs with salt, pepper and sugar. Place on a rack over roasting pan cover with foil and bake at 375° for 45 minutes. Combine, chili sauce, honey, onion, Worcestershire sauce and mustard in small saucepan and bring to a boil over medium heat, stirring constantly. Reduce heat and simmer 5 minutes. Uncover ribs and brush with sauce. Bake 45 minutes, brush with sauce every 15 minutes, until spareribs are fully cooked and tender. Serve with remaining sauce. Makes 4 servings.

∩

## COUNTRY HAM AND RED–EYE GRAVY

*8 slices country-cured ham*
*1½ cups water, divided*
*¼ cup black coffee*

Place ham slices, overlapping in a 15 x 18 X 2-inch roasting pan. The second slice in pan should completely cover the lean portion of the first one, continuing until all slices are in pan. Add ½ cup water and cover with large sheet of aluminum foil; press edges to seal. Bake at 350° for about 1 hour. Remove slices and skim off excess fat. Loosen brown particles clinging to pan and in same pan add 1 cup water and black coffee. Return to oven to reheat. Serve the red-eye gravy from the pan with ham slices. (Mary McFall)

# BAKED HAM

*1 (5 to 7-pound) smoked ham, fully cooked*

Heat oven to 325°. Place ham, fat-side up in roasting pan. Bake for 2 to 2½ hours (18 to 24 minutes per pound). Cut fat surface in diamond pattern to help cherry sauce penetrate and brush with cherry sauce. Return ham to oven. Continue baking, brushing with cherry sauce every 10 minutes for 30 minutes. Serve with remaining cherry sauce.

### Cherry Sauce:

*Water*
*1 (16-ounce) can pitted dark, sweet red cherries, drained, reserve liquid*
*½ cup sugar*
*1 tablespoon cornstarch*
*¼ teaspoon salt*
*¼ cup butter*
*1 cinnamon stick*
*6 whole cloves*
*1 tablespoon lemon juice*

Add water to reserved cherry liquid to equal ¾ cup in 2-quart saucepan. Combine sugar, cornstarch and salt and add to cherry liquid. Cook over medium heat, stirring occasionally, until sugar is dissolved (1 to 2 minutes). Stir in butter, cinnamon stick, cloves and lemon juice. Continue cooking, stirring constantly, until mixture thickens and comes to a full boil (3 to 5 minutes). Boil 1 minute. Remove cinnamon stick and cloves. Stir in cherry mixture.

**Washington, D.C. papers say: 'congress is deadlocked and can't act.' I think that is the greatest blessing that could befall this country.**

—*Will Rogers*

## HAM LOAF

1²/₃ *pound ground, smoked ham*
1⅓ *pounds ground pork*
*1 cup cracker crumbs*
¼ *teaspoon pepper*
*2 eggs, beaten*
*1 cup milk*
⅓ *cup packed brown sugar*
*1 tablespoon dried mustard*
¼ *cup vinegar*

Mix thoroughly meats, cracker crumbs, pepper, egg and milk and form into a loaf. Place on a rack in open roasting pan. Mix sugar, mustard and vinegar into a paste and spread over loaf. Bake at 350° for 1 hour or until done.

∩

## BRAISED VEAL CHOPS

¼ *cup flour*
*1 teaspoon salt*
½ *teaspoon pepper*
1½ *pounds veal chops,* ½-*inch thick*
*4 tablespoons shortening*
*Water*

Blend flour, salt and pepper together and roll veal chops in flour mixture. Melt shortening in skillet. Add chops and brown on both sides. Reduce heat, add small amount water, cover and simmer slowly until tender, about 45 minutes.

## FRIED FINS AND GILLS

½ cup flour
½ cup cornmeal
2 eggs
½ cup milk
4 fish fillets
Salt
Pepper
½ cup oil
1 tablespoon butter

Mix flour and cornmeal together. Mix eggs and milk in separate bowl. Salt and pepper fish. Dip fish in egg, then in flour. Fry in skillet with hot oil and butter. Cook over medium heat until golden brown. Good for trout, perch, catfish, sunfish and crappie.

No nation can accuse us of secret diplomacy. Our foreign policy is an open book, generally a check book.

—*Will Rogers*

∩

## CRUNCHY OVEN-FRIED FISH

1⅓ cups sour cream
1 tablespoon lemon juice
1 tablespoon chili powder
1 pound fish fillets
¾ cup finely chopped, corn chips
2 tablespoons butter or
margarine, melted

Mix sour cream, lemon juice and chili powder. Dip fish into sour cream mixture and coat with chips. Place in generously greased 9 x 13 pan and pour butter over fish. Bake uncovered at 500° for 10 to 15 minutes.

## BAKED FISH STEAK

1 teaspoon salt
½ cup milk
3 pounds fish steaks
½ cup dried breadcrumbs
4 tablespoons butter
Lemon
Parsley

Add salt and milk together and pour into a shallow dish. Dip fish into milk, then into breadcrumbs. Place breaded fish in baking dish and dot with butter. Bake uncovered at 450° for approximately 30 minutes. Garnish with lemon and parsley.

Ω

## FRIED OYSTERS

1 pint oysters, well drained
1 egg, slightly beaten
2 tablespoons water
½ cup cracker crumbs
½ teaspoon salt
¼ teaspoon pepper
Oil

Dip oysters in egg mixed with water, then dip in crumbs, salt and pepper. Fry in deep hot oil until golden brown. Makes 4 servings.

# JUST HANKERIN' FOR SWEETS

[pies,
pastries
and
desserts]

**Will Rogers with Henry Ford and his son, Edsel, enjoying the opening World Series game at Detroit.**

Franklin Delano Roosevelt spoke at the Hollywood Bowl during the campaign of 1932. When Will introduced him he called him Franklin, and said, "This introduction may not be very learned or flowery, but remember, you are only a candidate. When you are President I will do right by you, but I am certainly wasting no oratory on a prospect."

Will Rogers had a great deal of influence and was considered a great power in the political world. This fact did not go unnoticed by the Presidents of the United States. He met, performed for, or was friends with every President from Theodore Roosevelt to Franklin D. Roosevelt.

Will Rogers, First Lady Eleanor Roosevelt and Amon Carter in Los Angeles, California, on June 6, 1933, after flying together from New York.

Will Rogers introducing Franklin Delano Roosevelt at the Hollywood Bowl in 1932.

A great tradition is that of Will Rogers. He ought to be taught in the schools because of what he embodied of the best of the Constitution and the Declaration of Independence. He was homely as a mud fence and yet as beautiful as a sunrise over an Oklahoma field of alfalfa. There is a curious parellel between Will Rogers and Abraham Lincoln. They were rare figures we could call beloved without embarrassment.

—*Carl Sandburg, Poet*

Will Rogers with John D. Rockefeller in 1927.

"Ma" Ferguson, Texas Governor, Will Rogers, James E. "Pa" Ferguson.

[182]

Dizzy Dean,
baseball great,
and Will Rogers.

Will Rogers and
author Irvin S.
Cobb.

Will Rogers admired and liked Charles Lindbergh and from the beginning
there was an understanding between the two that developed into a close
and lasting friendship.

## ALICE'S BEST BUTTERMILK PIE

**Great!**

1 cup sugar
5 tablespoons cornstarch
2 cups buttermilk
3 large eggs, separated
Juice of 1 lemon
Zest of 1 lemon
3-4 tablespoons sugar
Dash salt
½ teaspoon cream of tartar
1 (9-inch) baked pie crust

Combine sugar and cornstarch in a 2-quart micro-wave-safe bowl. Add buttermilk and whisk to blend. Microwave on high for 6 to 7 minutes, stirring every 2 minutes. In another bowl, combine egg yolks, lemon juice and lemon zest. When microwave mixture is thick, pour some of it into the bowl containing egg yolks, lemon juice and lemon zest. Mix and then add combined mixture back into bowl with remaining filling. Cook about 1 minute. Remove from microwave, cool, pour into pie crust and set aside. Beat egg whites, sugar, dash of salt and cream of tartar into a meringue. Either spread meringue on top of pie or fold it into the filling. Brown at 325° for about 12 minutes. Serve at room temperature and refrigerate any left-overs.

This is a modernized version of my mother's recipe that is at least 60 years old. It is my husband's favorite kind of pie! During Bartles-ville's Mozart Festival, Café Keepsake serves lunch on the porch of the country store. Buttermilk Pie has become a favorite and has a "cult-ture" following! (Keepsake Candles)

## LEGEND CHESS PIE

*1 cup butter*
*3 cups sugar*
*6 eggs, beaten*
*2½ tablespoons vinegar*
*½ tablespoon vanilla*
*1 (9-inch) unbaked pie crust*

Preheat oven to 425°. Cream butter and sugar until no trace of graininess remains. Add eggs to creamed mixture and beat hard. Add vinegar and vanilla and beat again. Pour into pie crust and bake at 425° for 10 minutes. Reduce heat to 350° and bake for 30 minutes.

∩

## OKLAHOMA MINCE PIE

*1 cup raisins*
*3 tart apples, cored, peeled*
*½ orange, seeded*
*¼ lemon, seeded*
*½ cup sweet cider*
*1 cup packed brown sugar*
*½ teaspoon salt*
*¼ teaspoon cinnamon*
*¼ teaspoon nutmeg*
*¼ teaspoon cloves*
*2 (9-inch) pie crusts*

Put raisins, apples, orange and lemon through food grinder. Put in saucepan. Add cider. Heat to boiling, simmer 10 minutes. Add brown sugar and spices and mix well. Simmer 15 minutes. Measure, there should be about 2 cups. Pour into pie crust, put on top crust, seal edges and cut slits in top. Bake at 400° for 30 to 35 minutes.

**We are known as the wealthiest nation of all time. The difference between our rich and poor grows greater every year. You are either at a banquet in this country or you are at a hot dog stand.**
—*Will Rogers*

**[185]**

## BLUEBERRY PIE

5 cups blueberries, divided
1 cup sugar, divided
¾ cup water
1 tablespoon grated lemon rind
¼ cup water
3 tablespoons cornstarch
1 (9-inch) baked pie crust

In saucepan, combine 1 cup blueberries, ¾ cup sugar, water and lemon rind. Bring to a boil. Mix water, ¼ cup sugar and cornstarch and add to hot mixture. Cook until clear and thick. Pour thickened mixture over 4 cups blueberries in baked pie shell. Chill.

**Nothin', not even bad food, can ruin a Democratic dinner like some Republican sneakin' in.**

—*Will Rogers*

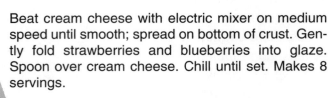

## DOUBLE BERRY PIE

1 (3-ounce) package cream cheese, softened
4 cups strawberries
½ cup blueberries
1 (14-ounce) carton strawberry glaze
1 (9-inch) graham cracker crust

Beat cream cheese with electric mixer on medium speed until smooth; spread on bottom of crust. Gently fold strawberries and blueberries into glaze. Spoon over cream cheese. Chill until set. Makes 8 servings.

## STRAWBERRY PIE

*1 cup water*
*1 cup sugar*
*3 tablespoons cornstarch*
*2 tablespoons corn syrup*
*2 tablespoons strawberry gelatin*
*3 drips food coloring*
*1 quart strawberries*
*1 (9-inch) pie crust, baked*
*Whipped cream*

In a saucepan, combine water, sugar, cornstarch and corn syrup. Boil until thick and clear. Add gelatin and food coloring. Cool and add strawberries. Pour into pie crust and top with whipped cream and serve.

**The crime of taxation is not in the takin' of it, it's in the way it's spent.**

—*Will Rogers*

∩

## AMERICAN APPLE PIE

*5 to 7 tart apples*
*1 cup sugar*
*2 tablespoons flour*
*1/8 teaspoon salt*
*1 teaspoon cinnamon*
*1/4 teaspoon nutmeg*
*1 (9-inch) pie crust*
*2 tablespoons butter*

Pare apples and slice thin and add sugar, mixed with flour, salt and spices. Fill 9-inch pie crust. Dot with butter, put on top crust and make slits in top. Bake at 450° for 10 minutes, then about 40 minutes at 350°.

## OLD-FASHIONED APPLE PIE
**1920's Recipe**

*1 (9-inch) pie crust*
*1 quart sliced apples*
*1 cup sugar*
*1 tablespoon flour*
*½ teaspoon cinnamon*
*2 tablespoons butter*
*½ tablespoon lemon juice*

Line a pie plate with pastry and fill with sliced apples. Mix sugar, flour and cinnamon and cover apples with mixture. Dot with butter and pour lemon juice over top. Cover with top crust and seal. Bake at 425° for 15 minutes and then reduce heat to 350° until apples are done, about 30 minutes.

∩

## RHUBARB PIE

*3 cups rhubarb, cut into 1-inch slices*
*1 cup sugar*
*½ teaspoon grated orange peel*
*3 tablespoons flour*
*Dash salt*
*2 (9-inch) unbaked pie crusts*
*2 tablespoons butter*

Combine rhubarb, sugar, orange peel, flour and salt and mix well. Pour into pie crust and dot with butter. Add top crust and flute edges. Bake at 400° for 40 to 50 minutes.

**I have always felt that the best doctor in the world is the veterinarian. He can't ask his patients what's wrong, he's just got to know.**

*—Will Rogers*

## EASY PEACH PIE

*1 stick margarine, melted*
*¾ cup flour*
*¾ cup sugar*
*¾ cup milk*
*1 egg*
*1 cup sliced peaches*

Heat oven to 375°. Melt margarine in a 13 x 9 x 2-inch pan and set aside. In a medium mixing bowl, combine flour, sugar, milk and egg. Pour mixture into pan with the margarine. Pour peaches into the pan and bake at 375° for 40 minutes. Crust will form on top.

∩

## NICE AND EASY PEACH PIE

*1 cup sugar, divided*
*2 tablespoons flour, divided*
*1 (29-ounce) can sliced peaches*
*2 (9-inch) unbaked pie crusts*

Put ½ cup sugar and 1 tablespoon flour in bottom of pie crust. Dip peaches out of juice and put on top of flour and sugar, then put the other ½ cup of sugar and 1 tablespoon flour on top of peaches. Use other pie crust for top crust. Cut slits in top and press edges of pie crust together. Bake at 425° for 10 minutes. Reduce heat to 350° and bake for 30 minutes. (Diane Reasoner)

**To be a good cook, you got to be either naturally an experimenter or just clumsy.**

—Will
Rogers

## OLD-TIMER'S PUMPKIN PIE

*1 ¼ cups pumpkin*
*⅞ cup packed brown sugar*
*½ teaspoon salt*
*1 teaspoon cinnamon*
*1 teaspoon flour*
*2 eggs*
*1 ¼ cups milk*
*1 (9-inch) pie crust*

Mix each ingredient, stirring after each addition. Put mixture in unbaked pie crust. Bake at 450° for 10 minutes. Reduce heat to 350° and bake about 1 hour.

∩

## PUMPKIN CREAM PIE

*1 (4¾-ounce) package vanilla pudding*
*3 tablespoons sugar*
*1 teaspoon pumpkin pie spice*
*1 (13-ounce) can evaporated milk*
*1 egg, slightly beaten*
*1 cup canned pumpkin*
*1 (9-inch) baked pie crust, cooled*

Mix all ingredients, except pie crust. Cook over low heat until mixture comes to a full rolling boil and remove from heat. Cool and pour into pie shell.

**Don't make the first payment on anything. First payments is what makes us think we were prosperous and the other nineteen is what showed us we are broke.**

—*Will Rogers*

## TRUE PECAN PIE

4 eggs
1 cup packed light brown sugar
¾ cup corn syrup
¼ cup butter, melted
¼ teaspoon salt
1 teaspoon vanilla
2 cups chopped pecans
1 (9-inch) unbaked pie crust

Beat eggs in a large bowl until foam and stir in brown sugar, corn syrup, butter, salt and vanilla. Sprinkle chopped pecans into pie crust and slowly pour egg mixture over pecans. Bake at 350° for 45 minutes. If top is browning too fast, cover loosely with aluminum foil during last 15 minutes of baking.

Ω

## CHOCOLATE PECAN PIE

¾ cup sugar
1 cup dark corn syrup
½ teaspoon salt
2 tablespoons all-purpose flour
3 eggs
2 tablespoons butter, melted
3 ounces unsweetened chocolate, melted
1½ teaspoons vanilla
1¾ cups pecan halves
1 (9-inch) unbaked pie crust
Whipped topping

Combine sugar, syrup, salt, flour and eggs and beat well. Add butter, chocolate, vanilla, and pecans. Mix well. Pour into pie crust, turning some of the pecan halves-rounded side up. Bake at 300° for 60 minutes or until the center is just set. Cool. Top with whipped cream. (Janet Orton, Oolagah Historical Society)

## CLEM'S WALNUT PIE
### Clem and Bart's Favorite Recipe

*1 cup white corn syrup*
*¾ cup sugar*
*¼ teaspoon salt*
*1 teaspoon vanilla*
*¼ cup melted butter, cooled*
*2 teaspoons lemon juice*
*3 eggs, slightly beaten*
*1 cup chopped walnuts*

Combine syrup and sugar, beating until well blended. Add salt, vanilla, butter and lemon juice. Stir in eggs and fold gently. Do not beat. Line bottom of 9-inch pie crust with chopped walnuts. Pour mixture over walnuts. Bake at 425° for 10 minutes, then at 325° for 35 minutes. (Donna [Mrs. Clem] McSpadden)

∩

## CONGRESS PARTY PIE

*1½ cups cold milk*
*1 (4¾-ounce) package instant vanilla pudding*
*3½ cups whipped topping*
*1 cup chocolate sandwich cookies, chopped*
*1 (9-inch) prepared chocolate pie crust*

Pour cold milk into large bowl, add pudding mix and beat until well blended. Let stand until slightly thickened. Fold whipped topping and sandwich cookies into pudding mixture. Spoon into crust. Freeze overnight. Remove from freezer about 10 minutes before serving. Makes 8 servings.

## SPECIAL TOUCH LEMON PIE

2 (8-ounce) packages cream cheese, softened
1 teaspoon grated lime peel
½ cup lime juice
1 can sweetened, condensed milk
1 crunchy pretzel crust

In a large bowl, place cream cheese, lime peel, lime juice and sweetened, condensed milk. Mix on medium high until smooth and pour into crust. Cover and freeze 6 hours. Let sit 10 minutes before serving.

∩

## ICE CREAM ORANGE PIE

1 (4-ounce) package orange flavored gelatin
1 cup boiling water
1 pint vanilla ice cream, softened
1 (9-inch) prepared chocolate crumb pie crust
Whipped topping

Dissolve gelatin in boiling water. Spoon in ice cream, stirring until melted and smooth. Chill until slightly thickened, about 10 minutes. Pour gelatin mixture into pie crust. Chill until firm. Top with whipped topping.

∩

## DEBBIE'S PINEAPPLE CREAM PIE

1 (4-ounce) package vanilla pudding
1 (15½-ounce) can crushed pineapple, drained
2 (9-inch) unbaked pie crusts
2 tablespoons margarine, melted
Sugar

Cook vanilla pudding according to package directions. Combine cooked pudding and pineapple and mix well. Pour into unbaked pie crust. Use the second pie crust on the top and seal edges. Brush with melted margarine, cut slits in top and sprinkle with sugar. Bake at 350° until golden brown.

> Trouble with our charities, we are always savin' somebody away off, when the fellow next to us ain't eatin'.
>
> —Will Rogers

[193]

## 5-MINUTE COCONUT PIE

*1 (3-ounce) package cream cheese, softened*
*1 tablespoon sugar*
*½ cup milk*
*1½ cups flaked coconut, divided*
*3½ cups whipped topping*
*½ teaspoon almond extract*
*1 (9-inch) graham cracker crumb crust*
*Toasted coconut*

Beat cream cheese and sugar. Gradually add milk and beat until smooth. Fold in most of the coconut, whipped topping and almond extract. Spoon into crust. Freeze until firm, about 4 hours. Garnish with toasted coconut. (Debbie Reasoner)

Ω

## GRANDMA'S CHOCOLATE PIE

*1½ cups sugar*
*3 tablespoons cocoa*
*4 tablespoons cornstarch*
*3 tablespoons flour*
*2 cups milk*
*4 egg yolks*
*1 tablespoon vanilla*
*2 tablespoons margarine*
*1 (9-inch) baked pie crust*

Mix sugar, cocoa, cornstarch and flour. Add enough milk to make a thick paste and mix thoroughly. Add remaining milk and egg yolks. Stir well and cook over medium heat until thick. Add vanilla and butter and stir well. Pour into pie crust. Top with meringue recipe above.

## MOM'S CHOCOLATE PIE

*2 cups milk*
*2 eggs*
*¾ to 1 cup sugar*
*1 heaping tablespoon cocoa*
*1 heaping tablespoon flour*
*1 teaspoon vanilla*
*1 (9-inch) baked pie crust*

Combine all ingredients and mix well. Cook over medium heat until thick and pour into baked pie shell. Top with meringue.

**Meringue:**

*3 egg whites*
*6 tablespoons sugar*
*¼ teaspoon cream of tartar*
*½ teaspoon vanilla*

Beat eggs until foamy. Gradually add sugar, cream of tartar and vanilla. Beat until stiff. Pour on top of pies and brown.

Ω

**Politics has got so expensive that it takes lots of money to even get beat.**
—*Will Rogers*

## MOM'S STRAWBERRY SHORTCAKE

*2 cups sifted flour*
*½ teaspoon baking soda*
*½ teaspoon salt*
*⅓ cup shortening*
*¾ cup buttermilk*
*1 quart strawberries, sliced*

Sift flour once and measure. Add baking soda and salt and cut in shortening. Add enough buttermilk to form soft dough and divide dough. Pat out or spread ½ of dough in 8-inch greased baking pan. Brush with melted butter. Place other half of dough on top of first and pat down evenly. Brush with melted butter. Bake at 475° for 20 minutes. (Mary McFall)

## CHERRY YUM-YUM

1 cup cold milk
1 teaspoon vanilla
2 packages whipped topping mix
¾ cup sugar
1 (15-ounce) can cherry pie filling
1 (8-ounce) package cream cheese, softened
1 (9-inch) graham cracker crust

Mix milk, vanilla and whipped topping together. Add sugar and cream cheese and beat well. Pour into graham cracker crust and top with cherry pie filling. Chill before serving.

## NO-CRUST COCONUT PIE

¼ cup margarine
¾ cup sugar
1 cup milk
2 eggs
¼ cup self-rising flour
½ (3½-ounce) can flaked coconut

Cream margarine and sugar. Add eggs, one at a time, mixing well after each addition. Add milk and flour, blending well. Add coconut. Pour into lightly greased 9-inch pie pan. (Makes it's own crust.) Bake at 350° for 45 minutes. Makes 6 to 8 servings.

## APPLE BROWN BETTY

*4 slices white bread, toasted*
*3 cups sliced, peeled baking apples*
*½ cup sugar*
*½ cup packed brown sugar*
*1 teaspoon cinnamon*
*¼ cup butter or margarine, melted*
*½ cup half-and-half cream*

Tear toast into bite-size pieces and place in a greased 1½-quart casserole. Top with apples. Combine sugars and cinnamon and sprinkle over apples. Drizzle with butter. Cover and bake at 350°. Serve with cream. (Mary McFall)

∩

## BANANA FRITTERS

*1¼ cup sifted flour, divided*
*½ cup sugar*
*1¼ teaspoon salt*
*2 teaspoons baking powder*
*1 egg, beaten*
*⅓ cup milk*
*2 teaspoons melted shortening*
*4 bananas*

Sift 1 cup flour with sugar, salt and baking powder. Mix egg and milk, and add to flour mixture gradually, stirring until smooth. Add shortening. Peel bananas and cut crosswise into halves. Roll in remaining flour, then cover with batter. Fry in hot deep oil at 375° for 4 to 6 minutes. (The batter is stiffer than for most fritters and requires a longer cooking time.) Makes 8 servings. (Jean Williams)

The Lord so constituted everybody that no matter what color you are, you require about the same amount of nourishment.

—*Will Rogers*

## FRUITY FRIED PIES

*1 cup milk*
*2 eggs, beaten*
*1 tablespoon sugar*
*1 cup shortening*
*5 cups flour*
*1 teaspoon salt*
*1 teaspoon baking soda*
*Fruit filling*

**You can always joke about the big man that is really big. But don't ever joke about the little guy who thinks he's somethin' 'cause he'll get sore. That's why he's little.**

*—Will Rogers*

Mix well all ingredients, except fruit filling. Take a small piece of the dough and pat out to the size of a saucer. Put 2 tablespoons any fruit filling, such as preserves, into dough, fold over and seal edges (no holes). Deep fat fry; then glaze.

**Glaze:**

*2 cups confectioner's sugar*
*⅓ cup lemon juice*

Heat confectioner's sugar and lemon juice until mixture comes to a boil, then remove from heat and pour over top of cake and spread on sides.

∩

## CRANBERRY–APPLE CRISP

*5 cups tart apples, sliced thinly*
*1 cup packed brown sugar*
*¾ cup flour*
*¾ cup quick cooking oats*
*1 teaspoon cinnamon*
*½ cup butter, melted*

Arrange apples in a baking dish. Combine sugar, flour, oats and cinnamon. Mix in butter until crumbly and press mixture over apples. Bake at 350° for 45 to 50 minutes

## APPLE CRISP

6 to 7 Granny Smith apples, peeled, sliced
1 (16-ounce) can whole cranberry sauce
¾ cup sugar
2 tablespoons flour
¼ cup chopped nuts
1 cup rolled oats
⅓ cup packed brown sugar
⅓ cup flour
1 teaspoon cinnamon
¼ cup butter or margarine, melted

Put sliced apples into a baking dish and set aside. Combine cranberry sauce, sugar and flour and mix well. Pour mixture over apples and toss to coat evenly. In a separate bowl, combine nuts, oats, brown sugar, flour and cinnamon, then add butter and mix well. Sprinkle over fruit mixture. Bake at 375° for 35 to 40 minutes. Makes 10 servings.

> **Farmers are learnin' that relief they get from the sky beats what they get from Washington.**
>
> —Will Rogers

∩

## CRAZY APPLE COBBLER

2 (17-ounce) cans apple pie filling
1 cup shredded cheddar cheese
2 tablespoons ground cinnamon
2 tablespoons sugar
1 (9.5-ounce) can refrigerator flaky biscuits
¼ cup margarine, melted

Spoon pie filling into a lightly greased 1½-quart casserole and sprinkle with cheese. Combine cinnamon and sugar and sprinkle 1 teaspoon of mixture over pie filling. Dip both sides of biscuits in margarine, then in remaining cinnamon and sugar mixture. Place biscuits on top of cheese. Bake at 425° for 15 to 20 minutes or until brown. Makes 8 servings.

## SANDY'S APPLE COBBLER

½ cup butter

2 cups sugar

2 cups water

½ cup shortening

1½ cups sifted, self-rising flour

⅓ cup milk

Flour

1 teaspoon cinnamon

2 cups finely chopped apples

Heat oven to 350°. Melt butter in a 13 x 9 x 2-inch baking dish. In a saucepan, heat sugar and water until sugar melts. Cut shortening into flour until fine crumbs form, add milk and stir with fork until dough leaves the sides of bowl. Turn out on lightly floured board. Knead just until smooth. Roll dough out into a large rectangle about ¼-inch thick. Sprinkle cinnamon over apples then sprinkle apples evenly over dough. Roll up dough like a jellyroll. Dampen edge of dough with water and seal edges. Slice dough into about 16 slices ½-inch thick. Place in pan with melted butter. Pour sugar syrup carefully around rolls. This looks like too much liquid, but crust will absorb it. Bake at 350° for 55 to 60 minutes.

∩

## DIANE'S PEACH COBBLER

1 stick margarine

1 (20-ounce) can sliced peaches

1 cup sugar

1 cup flour

⅔ cup milk

Melt margarine in baking dish. Pour sliced peaches with juice into baking dish. Mix together sugar, flour, and milk; mix well. Pour over peaches. Bake at 425° for 30 to 45 minutes. (Diane Reasoner)

## OLD-TIME CUSTARD
**1932 Recipe**

4 eggs
½ cup sugar
1 quart milk
1 teaspoon vanilla

Beat eggs with sugar. Add milk and vanilla and mix well. Place in shallow pan of boiling water, set in oven and bake at 350° until firm, but do not boil. Whole wheat bread or stale cake added to this makes a splendid pudding.

Ω

## LAST STAND CUSTARD

1 egg yolk
½ cup sugar
1 tablespoon cornstarch
2 tablespoons flour
¼ teaspoon salt
3 tablespoons cocoa
1 cup milk
1 tablespoon butter
½ teaspoon vanilla

In a mixing bowl, beat the egg yolk. Add the sugar, cornstarch, flour, salt, cocoa and milk and mix well. Cook over low heat until the mixture thickens, stirring constantly. Continue to cook for 15 minutes longer, stirring occasionally. Add butter and stir until butter is melted. When the custard cools, add the vanilla.

> Things in our country are not ever fixed, they just wear themselves out.
>
> —*Will Rogers*

[201]

## MELON BUBBLES

1 (4-ounce) package gelatin,
any flavor
¾ cup boiling water
½ cup cold water
Ice cubes
2 cups melon balls (cantaloupe, honeydew or
watermelon), divided

Dissolve gelatin in boiling water. Combine cold water and ice cubes to make 1¼ cups. Add to gelatin, stirring until slightly thickened. Remove any unmelted ice, measure 1⅓ cups gelatin into small bowl and add 1 cup melon balls. Pour into serving bowl. Whip remaining gelatin at high speed until fluffy and thick. Spoon over gelatin in serving bowl. Chill until set. Add 1 cup of melon balls to top.

## CHRISTMAS DESSERT

1 (4-ounce) package raspberry flavored gelatin
1 (4-ounce) package lime flavored gelatin
2 packages orange gelatin
1 pint whipping cream
1 tablespoon sugar
1 teaspoon vanilla
½ cup chopped nuts
1 small jar maraschino cherries
4 cups angel food cake pieces

Fix raspberry and lime gelatin according to package directions and pour into separate loaf pans. Let set all night in refrigerator. Mix the orange gelatin the following morning, let congeal and then whip cream, sugar and vanilla and fold into gelatin. Add nuts, cherries and angel food cake pieces. Cube raspberry and lime gelatin and fold into mixture.

## CHERRY PUDDING DELIGHT

1 (20-ounce) can cherry pie filling
1 (6-ounce) can crushed pineapple, drained
1 (12-ounce) can Eagle Brand milk
2 cups whipped topping

Mix all ingredients and chill in serving bowl.

∩

## HOMEMADE CHEESE CAKE

3 (8-ounce) packages cream cheese, softened
1 cup sugar
3 eggs
1 teaspoon vanilla
1 (9-inch) baked graham cracker crust

Beat cream cheese until smooth. Add sugar gradually; then eggs, one at a time and add vanilla. Pour into baked graham cracker crust and bake at 375° for 20 minutes.

∩

## POLITICIAN'S FLOP

2 cups flour
1 cup sugar
2 teaspoons baking powder
1 cup milk
2 tablespoons butter, melted
½ cup packed brown sugar
1 teaspoon cinnamon

Sift flour before measuring. Mix sugar, flour, baking powder and milk. Stir in butter and pour mixture in baking dish. Mix brown sugar and cinnamon and sprinkle over dough. Bake at 350° until brown. Serve hot with milk or cream. (Lorene Grant)

Have you ever been to a world's championship wrestlin' match? Us movie actors are advised to go there by our producers so we can learn how to act. Wrestlin' managers are overlookin' an extra big revenue, for folks would pay even more to see 'em rehearse with each other before the match.

—Will Rogers

## DOESN'T LAST DESSERT

*12 ice cream sandwiches*
*1 (8-ounce) carton whipped topping*
*2 large Butterfinger candy bars, crushed*

Line the bottom of a 13 x 9-inch glass dish with ice cream sandwiches. Spread whipped topping over sandwiches. Sprinkle Butter-finger crumbs over the top. Cover and freeze until ready to serve. Makes 8. (Shelley Plettl)

Ω

## HEAVENLY HASH

*1 cup butter, melted*
*2 cups sugar*
*4 eggs*
*1½ cups self-rising flour*
*2 cups chopped pecans*
*1 tablespoon vanilla*
*1½ cups miniature marshmallows*
*Chocolate topping*

Combine butter, sugar and eggs and beat slightly. Add flour and pecans, mix well and stir in vanilla. Spread mixture in a greased 9 x 13 x 2-inch pan and bake at 350° for 30 to 40 minutes. Sprinkle marshmallows over hot cake and return cake to oven until marshmallows are melted. Pour chocolate topping over hot cake and let cool.

## OLD-FASHIONED STRAWBERRY PUDDING

1 quart fresh strawberries
1 cup sugar
¼ teaspoon cinnamon
⅛ teaspoon ground cloves
1 tablespoon water
2 teaspoons lemon juice
⅓ cup butter or margarine, melted
1½ quarts ½-inch bread cubes
1 cup whipping cream

Combine berries with sugar, cinnamon, cloves, water and lemon juice in saucepan. Simmer for 3 to 4 minutes or until strawberries are soft and add butter. Toast bread cubes at 325° for 10 minutes. Blend with strawberry mixture. Pack into deep (1-quart) molded casserole. Cover and refrigerate overnight. To serve, unmold pudding onto a serving plate and top with whipped cream. Makes 6 to 8 servings.

## ∩

## FROZEN FRUIT DESSERT

1 (8-ounce) package cream cheese, softened
¾ cup sugar
1 (20-ounce) can crushed pineapple, drained
1 (10-ounce) package frozen strawberries with juice
2 bananas, quartered, sliced
1 (9-ounce) container whipped topping

In large bowl, beat cream cheese until smooth. Stir in sugar, pineapple, strawberries, bananas and whipped topping and mix well. Put in a 13 x 9-inch pan and freeze.

Us middle class never have to worry about havin' ol' furniture to point out to our friends. We buy it on payments and before it's paid for it's plenty antique.

—Will Rogers

# CHERRY PUDDING
## Will Rogers Memorial Gift Shop, Juna Phillips

*2 cups sugar*
*Pinch salt*
*2 cups flour*
*2 eggs*
*1 (16-ounce) can pie cherries, reserve juice, divided*
*2 teaspoons baking soda, dissolved in ¼ cup hot water*
*2 tablespoons vegetable oil*
*¼ cup water*
*1 cup chopped nuts*

Mix sugar, salt and flour. Add eggs and cherry juice. Dissolve baking soda in water, add oil and then add to egg mixture. Mix and fold in cherries and nuts. Bake at 350° about 45 minutes. Put on cherry topping before serving...

**Cherry Topping:**

*2 tablespoons flour*
*1½ cups packed brown sugar*
*¼ teaspoon salt*
*1½ cups hot water*
*2 teaspoons vanilla*
*2 tablespoons butter*
*Whipping cream, optional*

Mix flour, brown sugar, salt and hot water. Cook until thickened but not too thick. Add vanilla and butter and pour on pudding while hot. Serve with or without whipped cream.

## MR. SKITCH'S BREAD PUDDING
**Tammy Humburg, Secretary, Will Rogers Memorial**

*2 cups cream*
*6 slices day-old bread*
*1 cup sugar*
*1 teaspoon vanilla*
*1 teaspoon cinnamon*
*1 tablespoon butter, melted*
*3 eggs, slightly beaten*
*1 tablespoon flour*
*¼ teaspoon nutmeg*

Pour cream over bread and let soak for 10 minutes. Add all other ingredients and mix well. Pour into a greased 2-quart, baking dish and bake at 350° for 30 minutes or until top is golden brown. Serve with sauce.

**Sauce:**

*1 cup water*
*1 tablespoon cornstarch or flour*
*½ cup sugar*
*¼ stick margarine*
*1 teaspoon vanilla*

Combine ingredients and cook until thickened. Recipe may be doubled.

**Never blame a legislative body for not doing something. When they do nothing, they don't hurt anybody. When they do something is when they become dangerous.**

*—Will Rogers*

## FANTASTIC DESSERT
### Office of Secretary of State, Oklahoma, Kathy Jekel

*1 stick butter*
*1 cup flour*
*¼ cup confectioner's sugar*
*½ cup chopped pecans*

Melt butter and mix in flour, sugar and nuts. Press into a 13 x 9-inch baking pan. Bake at 375° for 15 minutes or until golden brown. Cool.

*1 (8-ounces) package cream cheese, softened*
*1 cup whipped topping*
*1 cup confectioner's sugar*

Mix well and spread on first layer.

*1 large box chocolate, instant pudding mix*
*1¾ cups milk*
*Whipped topping*

Beat until thick, about 3 to 4 minutes. Spread on second layer. (Spread immediately or mixture will become too thick to spread evenly.) Top with layer of whipped topping and sprinkle with chocolate shavings or pecans

∩

## CHOCOLATE-DIPPED STRAWBERRIES

*1 (½-pound) package chocolate candy*
*1 tablespoon shortening*
*1 quart strawberries*

Microwave chocolate candy and shortening at medium for 3 to 4 ½ minutes or until chocolate can be stirred. Dip strawberries in chocolate, one at a time and place on baking sheet lined with waxed paper. Refrigerate coated strawberries.

## CHOCOLATE MOUSSE

1 (6-ounce) package semi-sweet chocolate,
    grated, divided
1 (2-ounce) package unsweetened chocolate,
    grated
½ cup honey
2½ cups whipped cream, divided
¼ teaspoon vanilla
½ tablespoon sugar

Mix 5 ounces semi-sweet chocolate, all unsweetened chocolate, honey and whipped cream thoroughly. Heat in double boiler over hot water. Stir well. Slightly cool; fold in 2 cups whipped cream. Pour into 1-quart mold and chill. Add vanilla and sugar to remaining whipped cream and cover mousse. Sprinkle with remaining grated, semi-sweet chocolate.

Ω

## GOLDEN PECAN SUNDAES

1 pint vanilla ice cream
3 tablespoons butter or margarine
⅓ cup packed dark brown sugar
¼ cup golden raisins
2 bananas, sliced
⅓ cup chopped pecans

Remove ice cream from freezer; let stand at room temperature to soften slightly, about 10 minutes. In 10-inch skillet, over low heat, heat butter or margarine and add brown sugar until mixture is melted, stirring frequently. Add raisins and bananas and cook 5 minutes or until fruit is heated through, gently turning fruit. Spoon ice cream into 4 dessert dishes and top with banana mixture. Sprinkle with chopped pecans. Serve immediately. Makes 4 servings.

> On account of us being a democracy and run by the people, we are the only nation in the world that has to keep a government for four years no matter what it does.
>
> —Will Rogers

## LUSCIOUS PINEAPPLE ICE CREAM

*1 cup sour cream*
*1 (15-ounce) can sweetened, condensed milk*
*2 cups milk*
*1 (15½-ounce) can crushed pineapple, drained*

Combine sour cream and sweetened, condensed milk and add milk. Freeze in 2-quart ice cream freezer until partially frozen. Add pineapple and freeze firm. Remove dasher. Cover top freezer can with several thicknesses of wax paper, then replace lid. Pack in ice and salt. Allow to freeze 1 hour. Makes 2 quarts.

∩

## HOMEMADE ICE CREAM
**1930's Recipe**

*6 eggs*
*1 cup sugar*
*4 tablespoons white corn syrup*
*1 (15-ounce) can sweetened condensed milk*
*1 teaspoon vanilla*
*Milk to fill a gallon freezer container*

Beat eggs and sugar with an electric mixer, then add other ingredients. Pour into container, add milk to within 4 inches of top and freeze immediately according to freezer directions. After freezing, let stand packed in ice 1 hour before serving.

## MAMA'S HOMEMADE ICE CREAM

*4 to 6 eggs, beaten*
*2 cups sugar*
*1 gallon milk*
*1 teaspoon vanilla*
*¼ teaspoon lemon flavoring*

Mix all ingredients and put in ice cream freezer, ¾ full and freeze. Pack in ice and let stand 1 hour before serving.

∩

## TWO MILK SHERBET
**1930's Recipe**

*1 quart milk, divided*
*2 cups sugar*
*Juice of 2 lemons*
*Juice of 2 oranges*

Heat half the milk in a saucepan on low heat and add sugar. Stir until the sugar is dissolved, then remove from heat. Add the remainder of the milk and stir. Set mixture aside in a cool place. Press the juice from the lemons and oranges. When the milk-sugar mixture is very cold, add juice. Freeze at once.

∩

## CRUNCHY PRETZEL CRUST

*1¼ cups crushed pretzels*
*½ cup margarine or butter, melted*
*¼ cup sugar*

Mix all ingredients. Press mixture firmly against bottom and sides of pie plate. Refrigerate until firm. Fill as desired.

There is two things that tickle the fancy of our citizens; one is let him act on a committee, and the other is to promise him to let him walk in a parade.

—*Will Rogers*

**[211]**

## EXCELLENT PIE CRUST

½ teaspoon salt
2 cups flour
⅓ cup shortening
⅓ cup margarine or butter
⅓ cup ice water

Mix salt into flour. Work both shortening and butter into flour with pastry mixer or fork. Use small amounts of shortening at a time. Moisten dough with ice water by stirring with a fork. Pat into balls for 2 crusts; wrap in wax paper and chill thoroughly. This dough handles easily and bakes well.

Ω

## CHOCOLATE COOKIE CRUST

¾ cup flour
½ cup butter, softened
¼ cup confectioner's sugar
2 tablespoons baking cocoa

Preheat oven to 350°. Mix all ingredients until soft dough forms. Press mixture evenly in ungreased pan or pie pan. Bake until light brown. Cool completely.

Ω

## NO ROLL PIE DOUGH

1½ cups flour
2 tablespoons sugar
¼ teaspoon salt
2 tablespoons milk
½ cup salad oil

Mix all ingredients and press on bottom and sides of pie pan. Make edges rounded for a nice look. Bake at 350° for 20 minutes.

## BAKED PIE CRUST

*1 cup flour*
*3 tablespoons sugar*
*½ cup margarine or butter, softened*

Mix all ingredients thoroughly and press into bottom and sides of pie pan. Bake at 350° until edges begin to brown. Cool and fill with any filling. Makes 1 pie crust.

∩

## GRAHAM CRACKER CRUST

*1½ cups finely crushed, graham cracker crumbs*
*⅓ cup sugar*
*½ cup butter, melted*

Combine crumbs with sugar and blend with melted butter. Press firmly onto bottom and sides of 9-inch pie pan. Chill 1 hour or bake at 350° for 10 minutes.

∩

## SHORT-CUT HOT FUDGE SAUCE

*1 cup semi-sweet chocolate chips*
*¼ cup marshmallows*
*¼ cup milk*

Combine all ingredients in a bowl and microwave at medium for 2 to 3 minutes, stirring once during cooking. Serve sauce warm or cold. Makes about 1 cup.

> **It don't take near as good a man to be a candidate as it does to hold the office, that's why we wisely defeat more than we elect.**
>
> —*Will Rogers*

## HOMEMADE CHOCOLATE SAUCE

*½ cup butter or margarine*
*2 (1-ounce) squares unsweetened chocolate*
*2 cups sugar*
*1 cup light cream*
*½ cup light corn syrup*
*1 teaspoon vanilla*

In a saucepan, melt butter and chocolate. Add sugar, cream, corn syrup and vanilla. Bring to a boil, stirring constantly. Boil for 10-12 minutes. Serve warm or cold over ice cream or cake. Makes about 3 to 3½ cups.

**I admire any man that can rise above his surroundings.**
—*Will Rogers*

∩

## EASY CARAMEL SAUCE

*28 caramel candies (½ pound)*
*¼ cup half-and-half or milk*

Combine all ingredients in a small bowl. Microwave at high for 2 to 4 minutes or until caramel is melted, stirring every minute of cooking time. Makes about 1 cup.

∩

## ORANGE SAUCE

*¾ cup sugar*
*2 tablespoons cornstarch*
*¼ teaspoon salt*
*2 teaspoons grated orange peel*
*1 cup orange juice*

Mix all ingredients together in saucepan. Cook until thick and clear, stirring constantly. Makes 1¼ cups.

## OLD-FASHIONED CARROT CAKE

*2 cups sugar*
*2 cups flour*
*2 teaspoons baking soda*
*2 teaspoons cinnamon*
*1 teaspoon salt*
*1 ½ cups oil*
*4 eggs, beaten*
*3 cups shredded carrots*

Sift dry ingredients in bowl. Add oil and eggs and mix well. Stir in shredded carrots. Bake at 350° for 30 to 35 minutes. Spread icing after cake has cooled. (Mary McFall)

**Icing:**

*1 stick margarine, softened*
*1 box confectioner's sugar*
*1 (8-ounce) cream cheese, softened*
*½ teaspoon vanilla*
*1 cup chopped pecans*

Mix all ingredients well and spread over top and sides of cake.

**You got to sorter give and take in this old world. We can get mighty rich, but if we haven't got any friends, we will find we are poorer than anybody.**

—Will Rogers

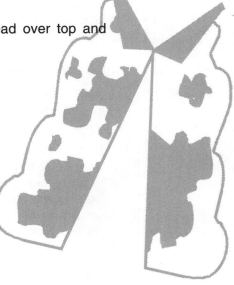

# PRIDE OF OKLAHOMA CAKE

*2 cups sugar*
*1 cup shortening*
*4 eggs*
*3 cups sifted cake flour*
*2½ teaspoons baking powder*
*½ teaspoon salt*
*1 cup milk*
*1 teaspoon vanilla*
*1 teaspoon almond extract*

Preheat oven to 350°. Grease and flour 3 (9-inch) round pans. Beat together sugar and shortening in large bowl until light and fluffy. Add eggs, one at a time, beating well after each addition. Sift together cake flour, baking powder and salt. Add sugar mixture to flour mixture a little at a time with milk, beating well after each addition. Blend in vanilla and almond. Pour evenly into prepared pans. Bake at 350° for 20 to 30 minutes. Cool layers in pans. To assemble: Spread tops of cakes with caramel filling and stack on cake plate. Frost sides with thin layer of butter cream and then again with thicker layer.

**Caramel Filling:**

*3 cups sugar, divided*
*¾ cup milk*
*1 egg, beaten*
*½ cup butter, softened*

Place ½ cup sugar in large saucepan. Cook over medium heat, stirring constantly, until sugar is light golden brown, about 5 minutes. Combine remaining 2½ cups sugar, milk, egg and salt in medium bowl and stir in butter. Add to saucepan. Cook over medium heat, stirring occasionally for 15 to 20 minutes. Cool 5 minutes and stir until well blended.

**Butter Cream Frosting:**

⅓ cup butter, softened
3 cups sifted confectioners sugar
2½ tablespoons half-and-half cream
½ teaspoon vanilla

Beat butter in large bowl until creamy. Gradually add confectioners sugar and then half-and-half until light and fluffy. Stir in vanilla.

**Congress is funny. A man gets up to speak, says nothing, nobody listens, then everybody disagrees.**
—*Will Rogers*

∩

# HOT FUDGE SUNDAE CAKE

1 cup flour
¾ cup sugar
¼ cup cocoa
2 teaspoons baking powder
¼ teaspoon salt
½ cup milk
2 tablespoons salad oil
1 teaspoon vanilla
1 cup packed brown sugar
2 tablespoons cocoa
1¾ cups hottest tap water

Heat oven to 350°. In ungreased 9 x 9 x 2-inch square pan, stir together flour, sugar, ¼ cup cocoa, baking powder and salt. Mix in milk, oil and vanilla with fork until smooth. Spread evenly in pan. Sprinkle with brown sugar and 2 tablespoons cocoa. Pour hot water over batter and bake at 350° for 40 minutes. Let stand 15 minutes. Cut into squares. Top with ice cream. ( Bob Plettl)

## DELIGHTFUL FUDGE CAKE

*⅔ cup butter or margarine, softened*
*1¾ cups sugar*
*2 eggs*
*1 teaspoon vanilla*
*2½ (1-ounce) squares unsweetened chocolate*
*2½ cups cake flour, sifted*
*1¼ teaspoon baking soda*
*½ teaspoon salt*
*1¼ cups ice water*

Cream together butter, sugar, eggs and vanilla until fluffy (5 minutes at high speed or mix 5 minutes by hand). Melt chocolate in double boiler, let cool and blend in chocolate to butter mixture. Sift flour with baking soda and salt and add to creamed mixture alternately with ice water, beating after each addition. Bake in paper-lined, 9 x 1½-inch round pans. Bake at 350° for 30 to 35 minutes or until done. Let cool and spread cake with fluffy chocolate frosting.

### Fluffy Chocolate Frosting:

*3½ (1-ounce) squares unsweetened chocolate*
*3 cups sifted confectioner's sugar*
*4½ tablespoons water*
*1 egg*
*½ cup butter or margarine, melted*
*1½ teaspoons vanilla*

Melt chocolate in mixing bowl over hot water. Remove from heat and blend in sugar and water. Beat in egg, then butter and vanilla. Frosting will be thin at this point so place bowl in ice water and beat until spreading consistency.

## CHOCOLATE SPOT CAKE

*1 box chocolate cake mix*
*1 stick margarine, softened*
*1 (8-ounce) package cream cheese, softened*
*1 box confectioner's sugar*

Make cake according to package directions and pour into a 13 x 9 x 2-inch pan. Then mix margarine, cream cheese and confectioner's sugar. Drop over cake mixture in globs. Bake at 350° for 1 hour.

∩

## ARKANSAS FOREST CAKE

*1 package chocolate cake mix*
*1 cup heavy or whipping cream, divided*
*1 tablespoon sugar*
*1 teaspoon vanilla*
*1 (21-ounce) can cherry pie filling, divided*

Prepare chocolate cake mix according to package directions. Bake in 2 (9-inch) layer pans. When layers are cool, in small bowl at medium speed, beat heavy or whipping cream, sugar and vanilla until stiff peaks form. To assemble cake, place 1 layer on cake plate and spread with half whipped cream mixture. Top whipped cream mixture with half of cherry pie filling, then with second cake layer. Spread remaining whipped cream over side of cake, spoon remaining cherry pie filling on top of cake. Makes 12 servings. (Dorothy Foster Bruffett)

> We pay all our congressmen the same salary. If somebody could figure out a scheme where each bird was paid accordin' to his abilities, we could save a lot of money.
>
> —*Will Rogers*

## CRUNCHY-TOPPED CHOCOLATE CAKE

*1 ½ cups flour*
*1 cup sugar*
*¼ cup cocoa*
*1 teaspoon baking soda*
*½ teaspoon salt*
*1 cup water*
*¼ cup plus 2 tablespoons oil*
*1 tablespoon white vinegar*
*1 teaspoon vanilla*

Heat oven to 350°. Stir together flour, sugar, cocoa, baking soda and salt in large bowl. Add water, oil, vinegar and vanilla, beat until batter is smooth. Pour into greased and floured 8-inch square baking pan. Bake at 350° for 35 to 40 minutes.

### Crunchy Topping:

*¼ cup butter or margarine, softened*
*½ cup packed light brown sugar*
*½ cup nuts*
*½ cup coconut flakes*
*3 tablespoons light cream*

Stir together all ingredients in small bowl until well blended. Spread on warm cake. Set oven to broil and place pan about 4 inches from heat. Broil until top is bubbly and golden brown. Cool in pan.

## MILK CHOCOLATE CHIP CAKE

1 box yellow cake mix
1 (4½-ounce) package instant chocolate
    pudding mix
1 (8-ounce) carton sour cream
¾ cup oil
3 eggs
¾ cup water
1 (6-ounce) package milk
chocolate chips

In a large bowl, blend all ingredients except chocolate chips and beat for 4 minutes. Fold in chocolate chips. Pour into a well greased and floured bundt pan. Bake at 350° for 50 minutes. Allow cake to cool before removing from pan. (Tyler Burgett)

> If they are going to argue religion in the church instead of teaching it, no wonder you see more people at a circus than at a church.
>
> —Will Rogers

## MAHOGANY CAKE

1 egg
1 cup sugar
1 tablespoon shortening
1 teaspoon vanilla
½ cup hot water
1 teaspoon baking soda
¼ cup sour milk
1 cup flour
2 tablespoons cocoa

Mix together egg, sugar, shortening, vanilla and hot water. Dissolve baking soda in sour milk. Add to sugar mixture and mix well. Sift together flour and cocoa and blend into sugar mixture. Blend and pour into greased, baking dish. Bake at 375° for 35 to 40 minutes or until done. (Mrs.C.H. Foster)

## POPCORN GUMDROPS CAKE

1 (16-ounce) package miniature marshmallows
¾ cup oil
½ cup butter or margarine
5 quarts popped popcorn
1 (24-ounce) package spiced gumdrops
1 cup salted peanuts

In a large saucepan melt marshmallows in oil and butter until smooth. In a large bowl, combine popped corn, gumdrops and peanuts. Add marshmallow mixture and mix well. Press mixture into butter 10-inch tube pan. Cover and refrigerate 5 hours. Dip pan in hot water for 10 seconds to unmold. Slice cake with a serrated knife. (Jessica Foster)

## LEMON POUND CAKE

4 eggs, beaten
1 package yellow cake mix
1 package instant lemon pudding
¾ cup water
½ cup oil

Beat eggs well. Add cake mix, pudding mix, water and oil. Beat at medium speed for 10 minutes. Pour into angel food cake pan. Bake at 350° for 40 to 50 minutes. Remove hot cake from pan and prick holes in top of cake. Dribble glaze over cake.

### Glaze:

2 cups confectioner sugar
⅓ cup lemon juice

Heat confectioners sugar and lemon juice until mixture comes to a boil, then remove from heat and pour over top of cake and spread on sides.

## FRUIT COCKTAIL CAKE

2 eggs
1/3 cup evaporated milk
1 1/2 cup milk
1/4 teaspoon salt
2 teaspoons baking powder
2 cups flour
1 (17-ounce) can fruit cocktail, undrained

In a mixing bowl, add all ingredients, mixing well. Grease a bundt pan, pour in batter and bake at 350° for 30 minutes or until done, then pour glaze over cake.

**Glaze:**

3/4 cup sugar
1/3 cup evaporated milk
1/2 cup butter
1 teaspoon vanilla
1/2 cup chopped nuts

Combine all ingredients in saucepan on low heat. Cook for 10 minutes and pour over cake. (Mary McFall)

> I don't care who you are, you just can't reach middle life without having said and done a whole lot of foolish things.
>
> —*Will Rogers*

Ω

## GENE'S DUMP CAKE

1 (15 1/4-ounce) can cherry pie filling
1 (15 1/4-ounce) can crushed pineapple, undrained
1 box yellow cake mix
1 stick margarine, melted

Mix cherry pie filling and pineapple. Pour into a 8 x 11 x 2-inch baking dish. Sprinkle dry cake mix over filling and pour butter over dry cake mix. Bake at 350° for 35 minutes. (Gene McFall)

## ANYTIME SPONGE CAKE

*2 eggs*
*1 cup sugar, divided*
*1 cup cake flour*
*⅛ teaspoon salt*
*1 teaspoon baking powder*
*½ cup milk*
*2 tablespoon butter, melted*

Beat eggs until lemon colored. Add ½ of the sugar at a time, continue beating. Sift together dry ingredients and add to egg mixture. Mix hot milk and butter together, then pour into flour/egg mixture. Pour into pan lined with wax paper. Bake at 350° for 30 minutes.

∩

## MISS BESSIE'S SPONGE CAKE

*5 egg yolks, beaten*
*1 cup sugar*
*1 tablespoon lemon juice*
*1 cup wheat flour*
*¼ teaspoon salt*
*5 egg whites*

To beaten egg yolks, add sugar, lemon juice and flour. Beat until well blended. Add salt to egg whites and beat until stiff. Fold into other ingredients. Bake in a tube pan at 325° for 1 hour.

## MRS. DAN FOSTER'S HICKORY NUT CAKE

**1932 Recipe**

*3 eggs*
*1 ½ cups sugar*
*½ cup butter*
*1 cup sweet milk*
*2 teaspoon baking powder*
*2 cups flour*
*1 cup chopped nuts*
*1 teaspoon vanilla*

Mix all ingredients well. Pour into a greased 9 x 13-pan. Bake at 375° until done. (Dorothy Foster Bruffett)

Ω

## EASY-QUICK APPLE CAKE

*2 cups flour*
*2 cups sugar*
*1 teaspoon baking soda*
*1 teaspoon salt*
*1 teaspoon cinnamon*
*2 eggs*
*1 cup oil*
*1 cup chopped nuts*
*2 cups cooked or canned apples, chopped*

Put all dry ingredients in a mixing bowl and mix well. Add eggs, oil, nuts and apples. Mix well. Pour into a greased and floured 9 x 13-inch cake pan. Bake at 350° for 1 hour.

> **Although the gamest women can keep back tears in sorrow, they can't keep them back in happiness.**
>
> —*Will Rogers*

# OLD-TIME YELLOW CAKE

1 cup butter, softened
2 cups sugar
3 eggs
2 to 2½ cups flour
¼ teaspoon salt
3 teaspoons baking powder
1 cup milk
1 teaspoon vanilla
½ teaspoon lemon flavoring

Cream butter and sugar, add eggs, one at a time and beat. Add flour, salt and baking powder, alternately with milk. Add flavorings. Bake at 350° for about 25 to 30 minutes or until done.

### Frosty Icing

2 cups packed brown sugar
½ cup cold water
1 teaspoon vinegar
1 egg white, beaten stiffly

Cook brown sugar and water until it forms a soft ball. Remove from heat and add vinegar. Pour over stiffly beaten egg white, beating mixture while pouring. (When pouring hot syrup into egg whites, pour a little at first to cook egg white, then add the rest.) Beat until thick and stands in peaks. Spread on cake.

# GRANDMOTHER'S FAVORITE WHITE CAKE

*2½ cups cake flour*
*1 tablespoon baking powder*
*½ teaspoon salt*
*½ cup butter or margarine, softened*
*1½ cups sugar*
*4 egg whites*
*2 teaspoon vanilla*
*1 cup milk*

Preheat oven to 350°. Line bottoms of two (9 inch) round cake pans with lightly greased, waxed paper. Combine flour, baking powder and salt and set aside. Beat butter and sugar in a large bowl at medium speed until light and fluffy. Add egg whites, two at a time, beating well after each addition. Add vanilla and beat until blended. With electric mixer at low speed, add flour mixture alternately with milk, beating well after each addition. Pour batter evenly into prepared pans. Bake 25 to 30 minutes. Cool and frost cake. (Marie Elifritz)

**The first sign of an impending resignation is a firm denial.**

—*Will Rogers*

## WATERGATE CAKE

1 box white or yellow cake mix

¾ cup oil

3 eggs

1 cup 7-Up or club soda

1 (3.4-ounce) package instant pistachio
    pudding mix

1 cup chopped nuts

Mix all ingredients. Pour in a sprayed 13 x 9-inch pan. Bake at 350° for 45 minutes.

### Cover-Up Icing

2 large envelopes instant whipped topping

1 ½ cups cold milk

1 teaspoon vanilla

1 (3.4-ounce) package instant pistachio
    pudding mix

½ cup coconut

¾ cup chopped nuts

Beat whipped topping, milk, vanilla and instant pudding together until thick. Spread over Watergate Cake. Sprinkle with coconut and nuts. Vary the icing by adding coconut and nuts to icing, instead of sprinkling on top. (Ellen Parker)

## OKLAHOMA DIRT CAKE

1 ½ pounds Oreo cookies
1 (8-ounce) package cream cheese, softened
1 cup confectioner's sugar
¼ cup butter, softened
2 (4½-ounce) boxes instant vanilla pudding
3 cups milk
12 ounces whipped topping

Place Oreo cookies into a plastic sandwich bag and crush with a rolling pin. Combine cream cheese, sugar and butter and mix well. Mix both boxes of instant pudding mix with milk and blend until thick. Add whipped topping to cream cheese mixture and add pudding. In large bowl, layer cookies, then cream cheese mixture. Keep alternating layers, ending with cookies (dirt) on top. (Martha Gilliam)

> **Nowadays every doctor has to have an accomplice. They travel in pairs and bunches.**
>
> —Will Rogers

Ω

## OLD MAW'S SPICE CAKE

2 cups sugar
⅔ cup butter, softened
3 eggs
3 cups flour
1 teaspoon baking soda
1 teaspoon cinnamon
1 teaspoon all spice
1 teaspoon cloves
1 cup buttermilk

Cream sugar and butter until light, add eggs and beat until smooth. Sift together flour, baking soda and spices; add alternately with buttermilk, starting with flour and ending with flour. Bake in 3 (9-inch) round cake pans at 350° or until done. Cool and frost with Butter Frosting

## PINEAPPLE UPSIDE DOWN CAKE

*4 tablespoon butter*
*¾ cup packed brown sugar*
*4 slices pineapple*
*4 maraschino cherries*
*1 ½ cups cake flour*
*1 teaspoon baking powder*
*¼ teaspoon salt*
*4 egg yolks, well beaten*
*1 ½ cups sugar*
*½ cup boiling water*
*1 teaspoon vanilla*
*4 egg whites*

**A debt is just as hard for a government to pay as it is for an individual. No debt ever comes due at a good time. Borrowing is the only thing that is handy all the time.**

—*Will Rogers*

Melt butter in skillet with brown sugar and cook until sugar is dissolved. Place pineapple slices in skillet. Place cherry in center of each pineapple slice and set aside. Sift and measure flour, add baking powder and salt and sift again. Beat egg yolks and sugar together and add boiling water. Add flour mixture and vanilla and mix thoroughly. Gently fold in egg whites. Pour cake batter over pineapple slices in skillet. Bake at 325° for 45 minutes.

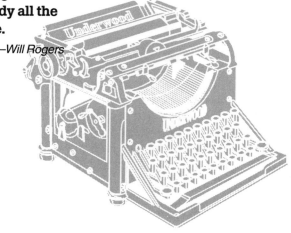

## SUGAR-FREE APPLESAUCE CAKE

*3 cups water, divided*
*1 ¼ cup raisins*
*2 ½ cups unsweetened applesauce*
*3 eggs, beaten*
*2 tablespoons sugar substitute*
*1 cup oil*
*½ cup water*
*3 cups self-rising flour*
*3 tablespoon cinnamon*
*¼ teaspoon baking soda*
*2 tablespoon vanilla*

Combine 2½ cups water and raisins in a saucepan. Bring to a boil and continue to boil until water evaporates. Remove from heat and add applesauce, eggs, sugar substitute, oil and ½ cup water and mix well. In another bowl, mix together flour, cinnamon and baking soda until well blended. Pour into liquid mixture, add vanilla and mix well. Coat a 10-inch bundt pan with cooking spray. Bake at 350° for 40 to 50 minutes and cool.

**The trouble with our praying is, we just do it as a means of last resort.**

*—Will Rogers*

∩

## COW PIES

*2 cups milk chocolate chips*
*1 tablespoon shortening*
*½ cup raisins*
*½ cup chopped slivered almonds*

On low heat, melt the chocolate chips and shortening, stirring until smooth. Remove from heat and stir in raisins and almonds. Drop by tablespoons onto wax paper. Chill until ready to serve. Makes 2 dozen.

# PEACH THUMBPRINT COOKIES

*½ cup packed brown sugar*
*½ cup shortening*
*3 tablespoon cocoa*
*½ teaspoon vanilla*
*1 egg*
*1 cup flour*
*¼ teaspoon salt*
*Peach preserves or jam*

Preheat oven to 350°. Mix brown sugar, shortening, cocoa, vanilla and egg in a 2½-quart bowl and stir in flour and salt. Shape dough by measuring tablespoonful into balls. Place on an ungreased cookie sheet 3 inches apart and press thumb deeply in center of each. Bake 8 to 10 minutes. Remove from cookie sheet and cool. Fill thumbprints with peach preserves. Spread with chocolate chip glaze. Makes 2 dozen.

### Chocolate Chip Glaze

*½ cup semi-sweet*
*chocolate chips*
*2 tablespoon butter*
*1 tablespoon corn syrup*

Heat chocolate chips, butter and corn syrup over low heat, stirring constantly, until chocolate is melted. Cool slightly and spread over Peach Thumbprint Cookies.

## OKIE SHORTBREAD

*1 cup butter, softened (no substitute)*
*⅓ cup packed dark brown sugar*
*⅓ cup packed light brown sugar*
*2½ cups flour*

Cream butter and sugars together and work in flour, then chill. Roll dough into a ½ inch thick sheet. Cut sheet lengthwise into strips ½ inch wide, diagonally 1½ inches apart to form diamond shapes. Bake at 325' about 30 minutes until lightly browned. Makes 5 dozen.

∩

## BUTTERFINGER COOKIES

*½ cup butter, softened*
*¾ cup sugar*
*⅔ cup packed brown sugar*
*2 egg whites*
*1 ½ cups chunky peanut butter*
*1 ¼ teaspoon vanilla*
*1 cup flour*
*½ teaspoon baking soda*
*¼ teaspoon salt*
*5 (2.1–ounce) Butterfinger bars, chopped*

Cream butter and both sugars. Add egg whites and beat well. Blend in peanut butter and vanilla. Combine flour, baking powder and salt, add to creamed mixture and mix well. Stir in Butterfinger pieces. Shape into 1½-inch balls and place on a greased baking sheet. Bake at 350° for 10-12 minutes. Makes 4 dozen. (Cindy Baughman)

I don't care how little a country is, they got a right to run it like they want to. When the big nations quit meddling then the world will have peace.

—Will Rogers

## ALASKA CREAM COOKIES

*2 cups packed brown sugar*
*1 cup butter, softened*
*½ teaspoon baking soda*
*1 cup sour cream*
*3 eggs, well beaten*
*1 teaspoon vanilla*
*1 teaspoon nutmeg*
*4 cups flour*

Cream sugar and butter. Dissolve baking soda in sour cream, add to sugar mixture and stir well. Add eggs, vanilla, nutmeg and enough flour to make a consistency that drops easily from a spoon. Drop by teaspoons onto greased cookie sheet. Bake at 350° for about 12 minutes. Makes 5 to 6 dozen.

∩

## OLD-FASHIONED SUGAR COOKIES

*1 stick margarine, melted*
*1 egg*
*2 cups sugar, divided*
*⅓ cup milk*
*1 teaspoon vanilla*
*2½ cups self-rising flour*

Mix butter, egg, 1½ cups sugar, milk and vanilla together in a bowl. Sift flour into mixture and mix well. Roll out and cut or drop by spoonful onto a cookie sheet. Sprinkle sugar onto cookies before baking. Bake at 350° for 5 to 10 minutes.

## MOM'S OATMEAL COOKIES

¾ cup margarine, softened
1 cup packed brown sugar
½ cup sugar
1 egg
¼ cup water
2 teaspoons vanilla
1 cup flour
½ teaspoon salt
½ teaspoon baking soda
3 cups oats, uncooked
Chopped nuts or raisins, optional

Beat margarine, sugars, egg, water and vanilla together until creamy. Combine flour, salt and baking powder, sift into creamed mixture and blend well. Place oats on greased cookie sheet and let brown lightly in oven. Stir browned oats into mixture and drop by teaspoons onto cookie sheet. Bake at 350° for about 12-15 minutes. Add nuts or raisins if desired. Makes about 5 dozen.

**There is no argument in the world that carries the hatred that a religious belief does.**
—*Will Rogers*

## DROP COOKIES

2 cups sugar
½ cup butter, softened
6 tablespoons cocoa
½ cup milk
3 cups quick oats
1 teaspoon vanilla

Put sugar, butter, cocoa and milk into a large saucepan and boil 3 minutes. Stir in oats and vanilla. Drop onto wax paper. Let cool and serve.

## COCONUT LACE COOKIES

1 egg
½ cup sugar
1 teaspoon butter, melted
½ teaspoon vanilla
½ cup oats, uncooked
½ cup chopped nuts
½ cup shredded coconut
¼ teaspoon salt

Beat egg until light colored and gradually beat in sugar, butter and vanilla. Combine with remaining ingredients. Drop onto greased, baking sheet and flatten with a knife. Bake at 375° until browned. Makes 2 dozen. (Tammy Long)

∩

## BEDROLL COOKIES

1 cup butter, softened
2 cups flour
1 teaspoon vanilla
½ teaspoon salt
1 cup chopped walnuts
½ cup confectioner's sugar

Cream butter and sugar together. Stir in other ingredients, except confectioner's sugar and mix well. Chill dough for 2 hours. Form dough into small balls, about 1 inch in diameter. Place on a greased cookie sheet and bake at 350° for 8 minutes or until done. Cool. Roll in confectioner's sugar. Makes 24.

## 1930'S GINGERSNAPS

*4 cups sifted flour*
*2 teaspoons baking soda*
*2 teaspoons cinnamon*
*2 teaspoons cloves*
*2 teaspoon ginger*
*1 ½ cups shortening*
*2½ cups sugar, divided*
*2 eggs*
*½ cup molasses*

Sift together, flour, baking soda, cinnamon, cloves and ginger and set aside. Cream shortening and 2 cups sugar together. Beat in eggs, molasses and sifted dry ingredients. Roll into 1-inch balls and dip in remaining sugar. Place on cookie sheet 2 inches apart. Bake at 375° for 15 to 18 minutes. Makes 4 ½ dozen.

∩

## OKLAHOMA CHEESECAKE COOKIES

*1 cup butter, softened*
*2 (3-ounce) packages cream cheese, softened*
*2 cups sugar*
*2 cups flour*
*1 cup chopped pecans*

Preheat oven to 350°. Cream together butter and cream cheese and add sugar, beating until fluffy. Add flour and beat well. Stir in pecans. Drop by teaspoon onto ungreased, cookie sheet and bake for 12 minutes. Makes 2 dozen.

**A woman brings a litle five year old girl up and says, "Tillie wants to meet you, she reads all your little articles in the papers and enjoys 'em." Tille says, "Who is he, Ma?"**

—Will Rogers

## POTATO CHIP COOKIES

*2 cups margarine, softened*
*1 cup sugar*
*3½ cups flour*
*1 teaspoon vanilla*
*1 cup crushed potato chips*
*¼ cup confectioner's sugar*

Cream margarine and sugar with mixer until light and fluffy. Add flour and vanilla and mix well. Add crushed, potato chips gradually, mixing well after each addition. Drop by teaspoons onto ungreased cookie sheet. Bake at 350° for 15 minutes or until golden brown. Cool. Sprinkle with confectioner's sugar. Makes 36. (Madison Plettl)

Ω

## BUFFALO CHIP COOKIES

*⅔ cup shortening*
*⅔ cup butter or margarine, melted*
*1 cup sugar*
*1 cup packed brown sugar*
*2 eggs*
*2 teaspoons vanilla*
*3½ cups flour*
*1 teaspoon baking soda*
*1 teaspoon salt*
*1 (12 ounce) package semi-sweet chocolate chips*

**It seems the more learned a man is the less consideration he has for another man's belief.**

*—Will Rogers*

Preheat oven to 375°. Mix shortening, butter, sugars, eggs and vanilla. Stir in remaining ingredients. Drop by teaspoons 2 inches apart onto greased, cookie sheet. Bake 5 to 7 minutes.

## COCONUT MACAROONS

1 (2-ounce) square chocolate
½ pound coconut
1 (12-ounce) can sweetened, condensed milk
1 cup chopped nuts
½ cup flour

Melt chocolate in double boiler. Add remaining ingredients. Drop by teaspoon onto greased cookie sheet. Bake at 275° for 20 minutes.

## COOKIES WITH A KISS

1¾ cup flour
½ cup sugar
½ cup packed brown sugar
1 teaspoon baking soda
½ teaspoon salt
½ cup shortening
1 cup peanut butter
1 tablespoon milk
1 teaspoon vanilla
1 egg
48 milk chocolate candy kisses
Sugar

Preheat oven to 375°. Lightly spoon flour into measuring cup and level off. In large bowl, combine flour, sugars, baking soda, salt, shortening, peanut butter, milk, vanilla and egg. Mix at low speed until stiff dough forms. Shape dough into 1-inch balls and roll them in sugar. Place 2 inches apart on ungreased cookie sheet. Bake at 375° for 10 to 12 minutes or until golden brown. Remove from oven and immediately top each cookie with 1 chocolate kiss, pressing down firmly so cookie cracks around edge. Remove cookies from cookie sheet and cool. Makes 4 dozen cookies.

> **Keep both parties out of office for one term, and just hire Henry Ford to run the whole thing. Then pay him a commission on whatever he saves us.**
> —*Will Rogers*

## STAN'S OATMEAL COOKIES

*1 cup shortening, melted*
*1 cup sugar*
*1 cup packed brown sugar*
*2 eggs, beaten*
*2 teaspoons vanilla*
*2 cups flour*
*1 teaspoon baking soda*
*½ teaspoon salt*
*3 cups oatmeal*
*1 cup raisins*

Cream together shortening, both sugars, eggs and vanilla. Mix in flour, baking soda and salt. Stir in oatmeal and raisins. Drop by teaspoons onto a greased cookie sheet. Bake at 350° for 8 minutes.

∩

## DOUBLE CHOCOLATE OATMEAL COOKIES

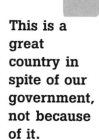

*1½ cups sugar*
*1 cup margarine or butter, softened*
*¼ cup water*
*1 teaspoon vanilla*
*1 egg*
*3 cups quick-cooking oats*
*1¼ cups flour*
*⅓ cup cocoa*
*½ teaspoon baking soda*
*½ teaspoon salt*
*1 (6-ounce) package chocolate chips*

**This is a great country in spite of our government, not because of it.**

—*Will Rogers*

Preheat oven to 350°. Cream together sugar, margarine, water, vanilla and egg in a bowl. Stir in remaining ingredients. Drop by teaspoons onto a greased, cookie sheet and place cookies about 2 inches apart. Bake for 10 to 12 minutes. Makes 5 dozen.

## PAT'S PEANUT BUTTER COOKIES

*1 cup butter, softened*
*2½ cups sugar, divided*
*1 cup packed brown sugar*
*2 eggs*
*1 teaspoon vanilla*
*2½ cups sifted flour*
*1½ teaspoon baking soda*
*½ teaspoon salt*
*1 cup peanut butter*

Cream butter, sugar and brown sugar with eggs and vanilla until creamy. Sift all dry ingredients together, add to mixture and mix well. Fold in peanut butter and mix together. Roll into 1-inch balls, criss-cross with a fork and sprinkle with remaining sugar. Bake at 375° for 10 to 12 minutes. (Pat Howell)

∩

## CANDY CANE COOKIES

*1 (18-ounce) package refrigerated, sugar cookie dough*
*Flour*
*1 (12-ounce) package white chocolate morsels*
*½ cup crushed candy canes*
*¼ cup chopped walnuts or pecans*

Preheat oven to 350°. Form dough into a ball and place on pizza pan or baking stone. Flatten slightly with the palm of your hand. Lightly flour dough and rolling pin. Roll dough into a 14-inch wide circle. Bake 18-20 minutes or until light golden brown. Remove dough from oven and immediately sprinkle chocolate morsels evenly over cookie. Let stand 2 to 3 minutes. Sprinkle with candy canes and nuts. Carefully loosen cookie from pan. Cool 5 minutes. Cut with pizza cutter. Makes 16 servings.

> **If women must insist on having men's privileges, they have to take men's chances.**
>
> —*Will Rogers*

## NUTTY CHOCOLATE OAT COOKIES
### Will Rogers Memorial, Carolyn Diffenbaugh

*1 cup margarine or butter, softened*
*1 ¼ cups packed brown sugar*
*½ cup granulate sugar*
*2 eggs*
*2 tablespoons milk*
*2 tablespoons vanilla*
*1 teaspoon baking soda*
*1 ¾ cups all-purpose flour*
*2 ½ cups quick oatmeal*
*½ teaspoon salt*
*2 cups semi-sweet chocolate chips*
*1 cup chopped pecans*

Preheat oven to 350°. Beat margarine and sugars until creamy. Add eggs, milk and vanilla, beating well. Add flour, baking soda and salt. Stir in oats, chocolate chips and nuts. Mix well. Drop by teaspoons on ungreased, cookie sheet. Bake at 350° for 9 to10 minutes for chewy cookies or 12 to 13 minutes for crispy cookies.

## MACAROON COOKIES

*4 egg whites*
*1 ½ cups sugar*
*½ teaspoon salt*
*1 teaspoon vanilla*
*1 (1-pound) package pitted dates, chopped*
*1 cup chopped pecans*

Beat egg whites until stiff, but not dry. Add sugar and salt gradually and continue beating until mixture holds shape. Blend in vanilla, then fold in dates and nuts. Drop by teaspoons onto greased, cookie sheet. Bake at 350° for 20 minutes. Makes 7 dozen

## MRS. ORAN STEWART'S BROWN SUGAR COOKIES
### 1932 Recipe

3 cups packed brown sugar
1 cup white sugar
½ cup shortening
1 tablespoon vanilla
½ cup butter
4 eggs, beaten
5 cups flour
1 tablespoon baking soda
1 tablespoon cream of tartar
1 cup coconut
3 to 4 teaspoons salt

Cream both sugars, shortening and butter, then add well beaten eggs. Mix flour, baking soda, cream of tartar, coconut and salt. Roll dough into a 3-inch diameter roll. Let stand in a cool place overnight. Cut in ½-inch slices and bake at 375° until golden brown. (Dorothy Foster Buffett)

∩

## NO-BAKE COOKIES

2 cups sugar
1 stick margarine
½ cup milk
½ cup cocoa
4 cups oatmeal
½ cup peanut butter

Bring sugar, margarine, milk and cocoa to rolling boil. Stir while bringing to a boil 1½ minutes, turn off heat. Stir oatmeal and peanut butter into mixture. When mixed well, drop from teaspoon onto wax paper and let cool. (Cindy Baughman)

> **Bankers are pretty sharp. They've come up with what they call 'holdin' companies.' That's where you hand the goods to an accomplice while the policeman searches you.**
> —Will Rogers

## SUGAR COOKIE SURPRISE

*1 (14-ounce) package caramel candies*

*⅓ cup milk*

*2 cups flour*

*2 cups quick-cooking oats*

*1 ½ cups packed brown sugar*

*1 teaspoon baking soda*

*½ teaspoon salt*

*1 egg*

*1 cup margarine or butter, softened*

*1 (6-ounce) package semi-sweet, chocolate chips, divided*

*1 cup chopped walnuts*

Preheat oven to 350°. Heat caramel and milk in a 2-quart saucepan over low heat, stirring frequently until smooth and set aside. Mix flour, oats, brown sugar, baking soda, salt and egg. Stir in butter with a fork until mixture is crumbly. Press half the mixture into a greased 13 x 9 x 2-inch pan. Bake 10 minutes and remove from oven. Sprinkle with half the chocolate chips and walnuts and drizzle with caramel mixture. Sprinkle remaining crumbly mixture over top. Bake until golden brown for about 20 to 25 minutes. Cool and cut into bars. Makes 40 bars. (Zach Earles)

## 1920s EASY WAY MACAROONS

*2 ⅔ cups coconut*

*⅔ cup sweetened condensed milk*

*1 teaspoon vanilla*

Mix coconut, milk and vanilla in bowl. Drop by teaspoon about 1 inch apart on well greased cookie sheet. Bake at 350° for 10 to 12 minutes or until golden brown.

## OLD-TIMER'S SUGAR COOKIES

*2 cups sugar, divided*
*1 teaspoon vanilla*
*1 cup butter, softened*
*3 eggs, beaten*
*4 cups flour*
*½ teaspoon salt*

Cream together 1 cup sugar, vanilla, and butter. Stir in remaining sugar and add eggs. Blend in flour and salt and mix thoroughly. Chill ½ hour. Roll out dough thinly on lightly floured surface. Cut out dough with cookie cutters. Sprinkle tops with sugar. Place cookies on greased cookie sheet. Bake at 400° for 12 minutes, until light brown. Do not over bake. Bakes 3 to 4 dozen cookies. (Tiffany Morgan)

## CRISPY CAKES

*½ cup butter, softened*
*1 ¼ cup sugar, divided*
*2 eggs, beaten*
*1 teaspoon vanilla*
*⅓ cup milk*
*2 teaspoons baking powder*
*½ teaspoon nutmeg*
*3½ cups flour, divided*

Preheat oven to 350°. Slightly grease cookie sheet. Cream butter with sugar, add eggs, vanilla, and milk and stir until smooth. Mix baking powder, nutmeg and 1 cup flour, add to creamed mixture. Mix until smooth. Add 2 cups flour and mix well. This will be a rather firm dough. Chill for about 30 minutes or until firm. Roll out on floured board into a thin sheet and cut with a large cookie cutter. Place on cookie sheet and sprinkle with remaining sugar. Bake for 12 to 15 minutes until edges just begin to turn dark. Cakes will become crispy as they cool.

**If all the time consumed in attending dinners and luncheons was consumed in some work, the production of this country would be doubled.**

—*Will Rogers*

**[245]**

# CHISOLM TRAIL BROWNIES

*1 ½ cups flour*
*¼ cup unsweetened cocoa*
*1 teaspoon cinnamon*
*1 teaspoon baking powder*
*½ cup nonfat sour cream*
*1 cup packed brown sugar*
*3 tablespoons honey*
*1 cup egg substitute*
*3½ teaspoons vanilla, divided*
*1 cup fat free cream cheese, softened*
*¾ cup sugar*
*1 tablespoon flour*

Preheat oven to 350°. In large bowl, combine flour, cocoa, cinnamon and baking powder and mix well. In a separate bowl, combine sour cream, brown sugar, honey, egg substitute and 1½ teaspoons vanilla, blend well. In medium bowl, combine cream cheese, sugar, flour and 2 teaspoons vanilla and beat with electric mixer until smooth. Pour cocoa brownie mixture into prepared pan. Top with cream cheese mixture. Swirl batters together using a knife. Bake for 35 minutes and check for doneness until knife inserted in center comes out clean. Cool completely and cut into squares. Makes 16 brownies.

## MUDDY BUDDIES BAR

*¾ cup margarine*
*3 eggs, divided*
*1 box brown sugar*
*2¾ cups flour*
*1 (12–ounce) bag chocolate chips*

Melt margarine in a small saucepan. Add eggs, one at a time, stirring after each addition. Add brown sugar, flour and chocolate chips and mix thoroughly. Pour mixture into a greased 13 x 9-inch pan. Bake at 350° for 30 minutes. Cool and cut into bars. (Linda Burgett)

Ω

## TASTY CHOCOLATE SNACK BITES

*1 cup rice squares cereal*
*2 cups semi–sweet chocolate chips*
*½ cup butter*
*2 tablespoons chocolate syrup*
*1 teaspoon vanilla*
*1½ cups confectioner's sugar*

Place cereal in large bowl. Line large tray with wax paper. Place chocolate chips, butter and chocolate syrup in medium bowl. Microwave at high until mixture is smooth when stirred. Stir in vanilla. Immediately pour mixture over cereal, stirring until all pieces are evenly coated. Pour mixture into large, recloseable plastic bag with confectioner's sugar. Shake until all pieces are well coated. Spread on wax paper to cool. Store in airtight container. Makes about 9 cups.

> It's the short memories of the American people that keeps our politicians in office.
>
> —*Will Rogers*

## FROSTED DELIGHTS

*1 ½ cups sifted cake flour*
*½ teaspoon salt*
*1 teaspoon baking powder*
*1 cup sugar*
*2 eggs, beaten*
*½ teaspoon vanilla*
*1 cup packed brown sugar*
*1 egg white, stiffly beaten*
*1 cup chopped nuts*

Sift flour, salt and baking powder together. Cream shortening with sugar until fluffy. Add eggs, vanilla and sifted ingredients and mix well. Spread batter very thin on baking sheet. Fold brown sugar into egg white, spread over cookie batter and sprinkle with nuts. Bake at 350° for 30 minutes. Cut into squares. Makes 30. (Linda Burgett)

## FUDGY BROWNIES

*¾ cup cocoa*
*½ teaspoon baking soda*
*⅔ cup oil, divided*
*½ cup boiling water*
*2 cups sugar*
*2 eggs*
*1 ⅓ cups flour*
*1 teaspoon vanilla*
*¼ teaspoon salt*

Stir cocoa and baking soda together. Blend in 1/3 cup oil. Add boiling water and stir until mixture thickens. Stir in sugar, eggs and remaining oil until smooth. Add flour, vanilla and salt and blend well. Bake at 350° for 35 minutes (Cindy Baughman)

## BLONDE BROWNIES

*½ cup shortening*
*2 cups flour*
*1 teaspoon baking powder*
*2 cups packed brown sugar*
*2 eggs. beaten*
*¼ teaspoon baking soda*
*1 teaspoon salt*
*2 teaspoons vanilla*
*¼ cup milk*
*1 (12–ounce) package chocolate chips*

Melt shortening and let cool. Mix together remaining ingredients except chocolate chips. Add to cooled shortening and mix well. Stir in chocolate chips. Bake in buttered, 9 x 12-inch pan at 350° for 35 minutes. (Nicole Davis)

**When I misspelled a few words, they said I was ignorant. Now that I misspell them all, they call me a humorist.**

— *Will Rogers*

## GREAT AUNT OPHELI'S DREAM BROWNIES

*½ pound butter*
*4 squares unsweetened baking chocolate*
*4 whole eggs*
*2 cups sugar*
*2 teaspoons vanilla extract*
*1 cup flour*
*1 cup chopped nuts, optional*

Preheat oven to 350°. Melt chocolate and butter in large bowl. Add, eggs, sugar, vanilla, flour and nuts and blend well. Pour into well greased and lightly floured, 11 x 13-inch pan. Bake for 20 to 25 minutes. Remove from oven. Cool and cut into desired size. If you do not let it cool completely, top with ice cream and get to eating. (Judy (Mrs. Jim) Rogers)

**[249]**

## WALNUT STICKS

*1 cup packed brown sugar*
*½ cup sifted flour*
*Pinch salt*
*¼ teaspoon vanilla*
*2 eggs, beaten*
*1 cup chopped walnuts*

Add sugar, flour, salt and vanilla and mix well. Add eggs and walnuts. Spread in greased, shallow 9 x 12½ -inch baking pan. Bake at 375° for 20 to 25 minutes. Cut into strips and remove from pan while warm. Makes 24.

∩

## ANYTIME FUDGE BARS

*½ cup butter*
*2 (1-ounce) squares unsweetened chocolate*
*2 eggs*
*1 cup sugar*
*1 teaspoon vanilla*
*½ cup flour*
*Dash salt*
*1 cup chopped nuts*

Grease 9-inch pan. Melt butter and chocolate in saucepan. Remove from heat and let cool. Beat eggs, sugar and vanilla together. Add melted chocolate mixture and beat well. Blend in flour and salt. Stir in nuts and pour into pan. Bake at 350° until smooth and slightly thick. Makes 1 dozen. (Shelley Plettl)

## DELIGHT BARS

*1 box lemon cake mix*
*1 egg, beaten*
*1 stick butter, melted*
*1 (1-pound) package confectioner's sugar*
*2 eggs*
*1 (8-ounce) package cream cheese, softened*
*2 tablespoons fresh lemon juice*
*Sugar*

Combine cake mix, egg and butter and mix well. Pat into bottom of a buttered, 9 x 13-inch pan. Mix sugar, eggs, cream cheese and lemon juice. Beat with mixer until smooth. Pour over cake mixture and spread. Bake at 350° for 40 minutes. Sprinkle with sugar and cut into bars. (Mary McFall)

**When you are satisfied, you are successful. That's all there is to success is satisfaction.**

*—Will Rogers*

Ω

## BIG BOB'S FUDGE

*3 cups sugar*
*1 ½ cups milk*
*7 teaspoons cocoa*
*2 teaspoons butter*
*½ teaspoon vanilla*

In saucepan melt sugar, milk and cocoa on medium heat, stirring often. Cook until fudge makes a soft ball . Drop a small amount in a cup of cold water to check. After fudge reaches soft ball  stage, take off stove and add butter and vanilla. Beat until firm. Pour on a buttered plate. Cut in squares. (Bob Howell)

## FIVE-MINUTE FUDGE

*⅔ cup evaporated milk*
*1⅔ cups sugar*
*1½ cups miniature marshmallows*
*1½ cups semi-sweet chocolate chips*
*1 teaspoon vanilla*
*½ cup chopped nuts*

Combine milk and sugar in saucepan. Cook over medium heat. Boil gently for 5 minutes, stirring constantly. Remove from heat, add remaining ingredients and beat until marshmallows and chocolate are completely dissolved. Pour into buttered pan.

Ω

## 1940'S THREE-MINUTE FUDGE

*1 stick margarine*
*2 cups sugar*
*¼ cup cocoa*
*½ cup milk*
*2 cups quick-cooking oats*
*½ cup peanut butter*
*1 teaspoon vanilla*

In saucepan, melt margarine, sugar, cocoa and milk. Bring to a boil, stirring constantly and cook for 3 minutes. Quickly add oats, peanut butter and vanilla and stir well. Drop by teaspoon on wax paper.

## REMARKABLE FUDGE

*4 cups sugar*
*1⅔ cups evaporated milk*
*1 cup butter or margarine*
*1 (12–ounce) package semi–sweet chocolate chips*
*1 pint marshmallow creme*
*1 teaspoon vanilla*
*1 cup chopped nuts*

Butter a 9 x 13-inch pan. Place sugar, milk and butter in saucepan and cook to soft ball stage (236°). Remove from heat and add chocolate chips, marshmallow creme, vanilla and nuts. Beat until chocolate is melted and blended. Pour into pan. Cool and cut into squares. Makes 8 dozen pieces.

Ω

## CALIFORNIA CHOCOLATE FUDGE

*2 cups sugar*
*1 tablespoon flour*
*3 tablespoons cocoa*
*⅔ cup milk*
*2 tablespoons corn syrup*
*1 tablespoon butter*
*⅛ teaspoon salt*

Combine all ingredients except butter and salt and cook to boiling point until a soft ball will form in cold water. Remove from heat. Add butter and salt, cool to luke warm. Beat until creamy. Pour onto buttered platter. Cut when cool.

It ought to cost as much to get married as it does to get divorced. Make it look like a marriage is worth as much as a divorce, even if it ain't. Besides, that would make the preachers financially independent the way it has the lawyers.

—*Will Rogers*

**[253]**

## SNICKERS FUDGE

1 (12-ounce) package semi-sweet chocolate chips
2 (3.7-ounce) Snickers candy bars, chopped,
    divided
1 (15.6-ounce) can creamy milk chocolate frosting

Line an 8-inch square pan with foil, extending over edges. Lightly spray pan with non-stick cooking spray and set aside. Melt chocolate chips in saucepan over low heat, stirring constantly, then remove from heat. Reserve 2 tablespoons of Snickers. Add remaining Snickers and frosting to chocolate chips and blend well. Spread mixture on foil-lined pan. Crush remaining candy bars and sprinkle on top. Refrigerate 1 hour until firm. (Sharon Wilson)

∩

## COCOA BEAN FUDGE

1 cup warm cooked pinto beans
¾ cup melted butter
1 cup cocoa
1 tablespoon vanilla
2 pounds confectioner's sugar
1 cup chopped pecans

Mash beans. Add melted butter, cocoa and vanilla. Mix thoroughly. Stir in confectioner's sugar gradually. Add nuts and press mixture into a 9 x 13-inch, buttered pan. Keep in refrigerator until ready to serve.

## MAPLE FUDGE

2 cups sugar
1 cup packed brown sugar
1 stick butter
¼ cup cream
1 tablespoon maple flavoring
1 cup marshmallow creme
2 tablespoons peanut butter
1 cup chopped nuts

In saucepan, mix sugar, brown sugar, butter, cream and maple flavoring. Cook on low 15 minutes. Remove from heat and add marshmallow creme, peanut butter and nuts. Beat until creamy. Pour into buttered pan. Let cool. Cut into squares.

Ω

## GREAT AUNT SOPHIE'S SUNDAY TRUFFLES

¾ cups heavy cream
2 cups chopped semi-sweet chocolate
confectioner's sugar, cocoa or crushed nuts

Heat cream in small pot until it reaches a boil. Immediately remove from heat, pour chocolate and cover with plastic wrap to allow chocolate to melt. Mix cream and chocolate together until smooth and refrigerate until it reaches the consistently of fudge. When cool, use a spoon or melon baller to scoop out the chocolate. Roll into firm balls with your hands. Refrigerate. To coat truffles, melt a small amount of chocolate and then roll each truffle in the melted chocolate and then in the coating of your choice: confectioners sugar, cocoa powder or crushed nuts. Refrigerate. Makes about 24. (Judy [Mrs. Jim] Rogers)

**We'll hold the distinction of being the only nation in the history of the world that ever went to the poorhouse in an automobile.**

—Will Rogers

## 1920s PEANUT BRITTLE

*1 cup sugar*
*1 cup light Karo syrup*
*1 ½ cups peanuts*
*1 teaspoon salt*
*1 teaspoon baking soda*

In heavy skillet put sugar and Karo syrup and stir until sugar is dissolved. Stir in peanuts and cook until light brown. Add salt and baking soda. Stir as little as possible. Let mixture bubble. When a small amount poured in cup of cold water, cracks, pour all on large greased, platter. When cool, break into pieces.

Ω

## MICROWAVE PEANUT BRITTLE

*1 cup sugar*
*1 teaspoon salt*
*1 ½ cups finely chopped nuts*
*½ cup light syrup*
*1 tablespoon butter*
*1 tablespoon vanilla*
*1 teaspoon baking soda*

Mix and microwave 4 minutes. Stir and microwave another 2 minutes. Remove from microwave and add butter and vanilla. Stir and microwave another 2 minutes. Add baking soda and mix. Work fast after adding baking soda because the candy will harden quickly. Pour onto buttered pan. Stretch with two buttered forks. Let cool and break apart.

## CHOCOLATE-COCONUT BALLS

½ pound sweet cookies, crushed
1 ½ tablespoons cocoa
1 ½ cups coconut, divided
1 (14-ounce) can sweetened condensed milk

Combine cookies, cocoa, and 1 cup coconut and mix well with condensed milk. Make walnut size balls and roll in remaining coconut. Makes 1 dozen

## PEANUT BUTTER CANDY

2 cups sugar
⅔ cup cream
1 teaspoon vanilla
1 cup peanut butter
1 cup marshmallow creme

In saucepan, cook sugar and cream to soft ball stage and remove from heat. Add remaining ingredients and beat until thick. Spread on buttered plate. (Sandy Frye)

**A diagnostician is just sort of a traffic cop to direct ailing people.**
*—Will Rogers*

## OKLAHOMA CREAM CANDY

3 cups sugar
1 cup light corn syrup
1 cup light cream
Pinch salt
1 cup chopped nuts
1 tablespoon vanilla

Combine all ingredients except nuts and vanilla in saucepan and stir over low heat until sugar is dissolved. Cook until soft ball stage is reached. Remove from heat. Cool without stirring. After cool, beat until creamy and add nuts and vanilla. Turn into a well buttered square pan. Cut into squares.

**[257]**

## CINNAMON CANDY

*2¾ cups sugar*
*¾ cup light syrup*
*¾ cup water*
*1 teaspoon cinnamon oil*
*8 drops red food coloring*

In saucepan, add sugar, syrup and water. Cook over medium heat and bring to a boil in about 7 minutes. Remove from heat and add cinnamon oil and red food coloring. Pour on buttered sheet pan. Let cool and break apart.

∩

## CARAMEL KISSES

*2 cups sugar*
*1 cup light corn syrup*
*1 pint whipping cream, divided*
*½ teaspoon salt*
*1 teaspoon vanilla*
*2 cups chopped pecans*

Butter platter. Mix sugar, corn syrup, 1 cup cream, salt and vanilla and cook, stirring constantly until thick. Add remaining cream in 3 portions, cooking until thick after each addition. When a few drops will form a firm ball in cold water, add pecans and pour into platter. When cool, cut into small squares.

## POPCORN BALLS
### 1920's Recipe

*6 quarts popped popcorn*
*1 cup molasses*
*1 cup sugar*
*¼ teaspoon salt*

Remove unpopped kernels from popped corn. Combine molasses, sugar and salt in a saucepan and stir to mix. Heat the mixture without stirring until the syrup is very thick. The syrup should reach 270°. If you do not have a candy thermometer, test the syrup by dropping a small quantity into cold water. If syrup becomes brittle, it is cooked enough. Put the corn in a large bowl so it can be stirred while the syrup is being poured over it. Dip your hands in cold water and shake off excess. Press corn into a ball. Repeat until all the corn is shaped into balls.

**Washington, D.C., the national joke factory.**

*—Will Rogers*

Ω

## SEVEN-MINUTE FROSTING

*1 ½ cups sugar*
*5 tablespoons water*
*1 ½ teaspoons corn syrup*
*1 teaspoon vanilla*
*2 egg whites*

Combine sugar, water and corn syrup in top of double boiler. Place over rapidly boiling water and beat constantly with mixer. Add egg whites and continue cooking and beating for 7 minutes or until frosting stands in peaks. Remove from boiling water, add vanilla and beat until thick enough to spread.

## BOILED FROSTING

2½ cups sugar
5 tablespoons corn syrup
½ cup water
2 egg whites
1½ teaspoons vanilla

Cook together sugar, corn syrup and water until candy thermometer reaches 240°. Beat egg whites until stiff, then pour syrup over egg whites and beat constantly. Add vanilla and continue beating until frosting stands in peaks.

Ω

## BUTTER FROSTING

4 tablespoons butter, softened
2 cups confectioner's sugar, divided
3 tablespoons milk
1 teaspoon vanilla

Cream butter, add 1 cup con-fectioner's sugar gradually, blending after each addition. Add remaining sugar, alternately with milk, until thick enough to spread.

Ω

## POWDERED SUGAR FROSTING

1 cup confectioner's sugar
¼ cup cream
½ teaspoon vanilla
¼ teaspoon almond
Pinch salt

Mix all ingredients in bowl until smooth.

# HOT 'N RISIN'

[breads and rolls]

# WILL ROGERS REMEMBERED

Will Rogers' telegram to his daughter, Mary, on the day of his death, August 15, 1935:

GREAT TRIP. WISH YOU WERE ALL ALONG. HOW'S YOUR ACTING? YOU AND MAMA WIRE ME ALL THE NEWS TO NOME. GOING TO POINT BARROW TODAY. FURTHEST POINT OF LAND ON WHOLE AMERICAN CONTI-NENT. LOTS OF LOVE. DON'T WORRY. DAD

On August 15, 1935, in spite of bad weather, Will Rogers and Wiley Post took off from Fairbanks, Alaska, for Point Barrow, Alaska, the northernmost point of land on the North Ameri-can continent. Several hours later they landed on a lagoon where some Eskimos were fishing. They found out they were only about fifteen miles from Barrow. They took off, climbed about 100 feet in the air and banked sharply to the right. The engine sputtered twice and died—the red plane dived nose first into the bay. Will Rogers and Wiley Post were killed instantly.

Congress voted $500,000 for a memorial to Will

**His departure was a loss not only to those who were close to him, but to everyone who came in contact with the great comfort of his way of creating a bright day out of one that had all appearances of a dark one. I lost a friend.**

—*Tom Mix, Cowboy Movie Star*

Rogers after he was killed, but President Franklin D. Roosevelt vetoed it. He felt that the money could be better used by a nation just coming out of a terrible depression—and knew that Will would have agreed with him. Private donations were used to establish scholarships at universities in Oklahoma, Texas and California.

**Will Rogers and Wiley Post, about two hours before their fatal flight from Fairbanks to Pt. Barrow, Alaska, August 15, 1935.**

**I have lost a dear friend.**

*Charlie Chaplin,*
*Actor*

**Will Rogers had great affection and admiration for Wiley Post, a fellow Oklahoman, and felt that his achievements had never been properly recognized.**

Oklahoma City, Oklahoma, is the only city in the world with two airports named for people who died in a plane crash: Will Rogers World Airport and Wiley Post General Aviation Airport.

**He dignified the virtues of every honest American by winning the admiration and fondness of kings and queens, as well as that of the humblest folk who walk this earth. No man alive in our time ever had so many friends.**

*—Cecil B. DeMille, Motion Picture Producer*

**Will Rogers and Wiley Post in Alaska shortly before their fatal flight.**

When the National Cowboy Hall of Fame and Western Heritage Center was founded by seventeen western states, Will Rogers was the first to be unanimously voted into it.
At Colorado Springs, Colorado,

> **This generation so much needed the example of Will's life and writings, and his passing is an irreparable loss to the nation.**
>
> —*Harvey S. Firestone*

on the eastern slopes of the Rocky Mountains, pointing like a finger toward heaven, stands the Will Rogers Shrine. Every fifteen minutes chimes play and can be heard up to twenty miles away—easily carrying to the nearby United States Air Force Academy. Will was a pioneer in aviation-advocating    a strong Air Force. The Committee on Awards of The "Spirit of St. Louis" Aeronautical Medal voted on July 17 that Will Rogers was the outstanding logical person to receive the award for 1935. It was presented to his widow, Mrs. Betty Rogers, on October 11, 1935.

Will Rogers was named to the Aviation Hall of Fame in Dayton, Ohio, in 1977. Actor James Stewart presented the award.

Will Rogers flew over half a million miles all over the world at a time when aviation was still in its trial-and-error period. The confidence he showed in the future of air travel and the columns he wrote about it were a strong factor in the development of commercial aviation.

This statue of Will Rogers by Jo Davidson stands in the rotunda of the Will Rogers Memorial in Claremore, Oklahoma and in Statuary Hall in our nation's Capitol. He is the only humorist so honored. Before he died, Will said, "If they ever put up a statue of me, I want it to face Congress, because I want to keep an eye on them birds." It is placed in the hallway, outside the rotunda, facing the House of Congress.

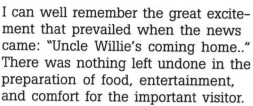

I can well remember the great excitement that prevailed when the news came: "Uncle Willie's coming home.." There was nothing left undone in the preparation of food, entertainment, and comfort for the important visitor.

Sharing was the Rogers' way and between visits we were not forgotten. There were letters, rare and distinctive gifts, clippings, the latest sheet music and always a wealth of postal cards from all over the country and foreign lands.

No matter where Uncle Will was playing he always sent for some of the family to join him. And he wanted to be included in anything that affected the family. He always came when he could if there was illness or death.

—*Paula McSpadden Love, Will's niece and first curator of the Will Rogers Memorial*

**Will Rogers and Henry Ford, automobile tycoon.**

**Our greatest thrill since entering radio was not while in a broadcasting studio, but at home listening to a radio program and hearing Will Rogers imitate Amos 'n' Andy. It was by far the best we ever heard, yet in a wire Rogers sent us the following morning he not only apologized for his imitation, but referred to it as, "A bum job."**

—*Amos 'n' Andy, famous radio personalities*

August 16, 1935. Shirley Temple, Hollywood's youngest top notch star, broke into tears today when she learned the news of Will Rogers' death. The child was a favorite of Rogers and frequently the two "cut up together." Crying bitterly, Shirley said, "I hate airplanes!"

**Will has left the whole world enriched. His splendid life shall stand always an inspiration to us.**

*—Laurel and Hardy,*
*Comedians*

The man with the warmest heart flew into Arctic space.

Will Rogers, Jr., Will Rogers, Billie Burk, Wiley Post and Fred Stone.

Although the plane in which he rode fell in one of the most tragic accidents of modern times, it could not destroy its immortal cargo. Will Rogers can never die.

**Few geniuses in the history of the world have been able to use laughter for moral guidance, for the shaping and stimulating of national thought and a people's perspective. Will Rogers was an apostle of laughter and common sense. And to make his genius utterly unique, Will had the God-given gift of removing the sting from his remarks.**

*—Cecil B. DeMille, Motion Picture Producer*

**A smile has disappeared from the lips of America and her eyes are now suffused with tears. He was a man, we shall not look upon his like again.**

—*John McCormack, Irish Tenor and Will Rogers' friend*

There are many streams, but only here and there a great Mississippi; There are many echoes, but only now and then an original voice; There are many musicians, but only now and then a Mendelssohn or Mozart; There are many people, but only now and then an outstanding individual.

—*Rev. Dr. James Whitcomb Brougher, Sr. (Will Rogers' Eulogy)*

Shirley Temple visits Will Rogers at the Fox lot during the shooting of *David Harum* in 1934.

**If Will Rogers were not one of the most talented men of his time, he would have achieved greatness for this simple statement in a world swollen and angry red with hate: "I NEVER MET A MAN I DIDN'T LIKE."**

—*Odd McIntyre, Newspaperman and pal of Will Rogers*

We pay grateful homage to the memory of a man who helped the nation to smile...Will Rogers' humor and his comments were always kind. His was no biting sarcasm that hurt the highest or the lowest of his fellow citizens. When he wanted people to laugh out loud he used the methods of pure fun. And when he wanted to make a point for the good of all mankind, he used the kind of gentle irony that left no scars behind it...From him we can learn anew the homely lesson that the way to progress is to build on what we have, to believe that today is better than yesterday and that tomorrow will be better than either...

The American nation, to whose heart he brought gladness, will hold him in everlasting remembrance.

—*Franklin D. Roosevelt, President of the United States*

Will Rogers, Amon Carter, Tris Speaker, baseball player, in Fort Worth Texas, in 1925.

**He was unspoiled by fame and fortune. He could walk with kings and keep the common touch. He was America's greatest humorist. He had more than humor, he had a heart; more than talent, he had genius. Genius is universal, it is not national, it is not local, it belongs to no time or place. It belongs to the race. It is the heritage of man.**

—*Senator Thomas P. Gore, Oklahoma*

The English speaking world has lost one of its kindliest personalities, well named Ambassador of Good Will.

—*W. J. Hutchinson of London, England*

**Will Rogers cannot die any more than Mark Twain could.**

—*Spencer Tracy, Actor*

## HOMEMADE BREAD

*1 tablespoon yeast*
*1 quart lukewarm water*
*2 tablespoons sugar*
*2 teaspoons salt*
*½ cup mashed potatoes*
*2 tablespoons oil*
*Flour*

**Civilization has taught us to eat with a fork, but even now if nobody is around we use our fingers.**

—Will Rogers

Dissolve yeast in lukewarm water and add sugar, salt, mashed potatoes and oil. Mix well. Work in flour until it does not stick to your hands.. Let rise for 3 hours. Punch down and let rise 1½ hours. Put in greased loaf pan. Bake at 350° until brown.

## HOMESPUN BREAD

*3 cups lukewarm water*
*3 packages dry yeast*
*3 tablespoons sugar*
*¼ cup shortening, melted*
*1 tablespoon salt*
*5½ cups flour, divided*
*1 egg*
*1 tablespoon water*

Put warm water in a big mixing bowl. Add yeast and sugar. Let stand about 10 minutes, then add shortening, salt and enough flour to make a soft sponge. Beat well, then knead in the rest of the flour. Let rise until double in bulk. Make 3 long narrow loaves. Let rise again. Now make 3 cuts crosswise across the top of the loaves and brush the loaves with a mixture of 1 egg and 1 tablespoon water beaten together. Bake at 350° for 45 minutes.

## CHEDDAR CHEESE BREAD

½ cup boiling water
1½ teaspoon salt
¼ cup sugar
3 tablespoon shortening
½ cup evaporated milk
1 package yeast
¼ cup lukewarm water
2 eggs, beaten
3½ cups flour, divided
1 cup shredded sharp cheddar cheese

**You must judge a man's greatness by how much he will be missed.**

—Will Rogers

Combine boiling water, salt, sugar, and shortening in a medium mixing bowl. Stir until shortening is melted and add milk. Dissolve yeast in lukewarm water and add to sugar mixture when cooled to lukewarm. Stir in eggs, one at a time. Add about half the flour and beat well. Add remaining flour and beat until smooth. Let dough rise about 1 hour and 30 minutes or until doubled in bulk. Meanwhile, grease two small loaf pans and set aside. Add cheese to dough and mix well. Divide dough in half and spread on bottom of the pans. Let rise for about 1 hour or until doubled in bulk. Bake at 400° for 20 to 25 minutes or until bread is golden brown. Makes 2 small loaves.

## HOMEMADE CHEESE BREAD

*1 tablespoon sugar*
*1 teaspoon salt*
*⅔ cup lukewarm water*
*1 cake yeast*
*1 egg, well beaten*
*1⅓ cups grated American cheese*
*2⅓ cups sifted flour*

Dissolve sugar and salt in lukewarm water. Crumble in yeast and stir until dissolved. Add beaten egg, grated cheese and flour to make easily handled dough. Knead dough quickly and lightly until smooth and elastic. Shape into loaf and place into greased bread pans. Cover and let rise in warm place, until doubled in bulk, about 1¾ hours. Bake at 375° for 45 minutes.

Ω

## INDIAN BEAN BREAD
### Will Rogers Memorial Librarian Pat Lowe

*2 cups oatmeal*
*1 teaspoon salt*
*1 teaspoon baking powder*
*2 eggs, beaten*
*1½ cups milk*
*2 cups cooked brown beans*

Mix together all dry ingredients, then add eggs and milk. Stir in brown beans. Pour into a greased iron skillet. Bake at 450° for 25 minutes or until brown.

## INDIAN FRY BREAD

*3 cups oil*
*6½ cups self-rising flour*
*2½ cups warm water*

Preheat oil in an iron skillet or deep fryer to 450°. Pour 6 cups flour into a large mixing bowl. Make a well in center and add the warm water a little at a time. Mix until dough can be handled. Knead until it loses its stickiness and cover for 15 minutes. Sprinkle flour on board and pinch a piece of dough the size of a small orange. Place on floured board and pat until ⅛ inch thick. Drop into hot oil. Turn once. Remove from oil with slotted spoon when brown. Punch a hole to remove air. Drain on paper towel. Makes 18.

∩

## SQUAW BREAD

*1 pint sour cream*
*1 tablespoon shortening*
*3 heaping teaspoons baking powder*
*1 teaspoon salt*
*½ teaspoon soda*
*Flour*
*Oil*

Mix sour cream, shortening, baking powder, salt and baking soda well. Add enough flour to make dough easy to handle. Knead it until smooth and roll out until dough is about ½-inch thick. Divide into strips and make slits in them. Cook in deep oil just like doughnuts.

When I die, my epitaph, or whatever you call those signs on gravestones, is gonna read, 'I joked about every prominent man of my time, but I never met a man I didn't like.' I'm so proud of that I can hardly wait to die so it can be carved. And when you come to my grave, you'll probably find me sittin' there proudly readin' it.

—*Will Rogers*

## SQUAW ROLL BREAD

*2 cups flour*
*1½ teaspoons sugar*
*4 teaspoons baking powder*
*½ teaspoon milk*
*Oil*

> **We are all just hangin' on here as long as we can. I don't know why we hate to go. We know it's better there. Maybe it's because we haven't done anything that will live after we are gone.**
>
> —*Will Rogers*

Mix flour, sugar and baking powder. Pour in milk and mix well. Roll out like biscuits, cut in 2 x 4-inch pieces and slit center to let out steam. Fry in deep oil until golden brown.

Ω

## SCOTT'S CHEESE BREAD

*2 cups buttermilk baking mix*
*½ cup shredded processed sharp American cheese*
*⅔ cup milk*

Preheat oven to 450°. Grease 2½ x 1¼-inch muffin cups. Mix all ingredients until soft dough forms. Drop dough by spoonfuls into muffin cups. Bake until muffins are light brown, 10-15 minutes.

Ω

## CHOPPED CHILI CHEESE BREAD

*1 (8-ounce) jar cheese spread*
*1 (4-ounce) can chopped green chilies, drained*
*1 (1-pound) loaf Italian bread*

Mix cheese spread and chilies. Cut loaf diagonally into 1-inch slices to within ½ inch of bottom. Spread both sides of each slice with cheese mixture. Place loaf on an 18x18 inch slice of aluminum foil. Bring foil up around loaf, pressing against sides and leaving top uncovered. Heat in 350° oven until hot and crusty, about 20 minutes.

## PARMESAN BREAD

*1½ cups buttermilk baking mix*
*1 egg*
*¼ cup sliced green onion, with tops*
*¼ cup milk*
*¼ cup apple juice*
*1 tablespoon sugar*
*½ teaspoon dried tarragon*
*¼ cup grated Parmesan cheese*

Preheat oven to 400°. Grease 8 x 1½-inch round baking pan. Mix all ingredients except cheese and beat vigorously 30 seconds. Spread in pan and sprinkle with cheese. Bake until golden brown, 20 to 25 minutes. Cut into wedges. Makes 8 wedges.

∩

## GINGER BREAD
**1932 Recipe**

*1 egg*
*1 cup molasses*
*1 cup sugar*
*1 cup thick sour cream*
*1 teaspoon soda*
*1 teaspoon baking powder*
*1 teaspoon ginger*
*Flour*

Mix egg, molasses, sugar, sour cream, baking soda, baking powder and ginger. Work in flour until it does not stick to your hand. Do not make too thick. Bake at 375° until toothpick stuck in center of bread comes out clean. (Mrs. W.F. Stephen)

## HUCKLEBERRY BREAD
### Cherokee National Historical Society

*1 stick butter, softened*
*1 cup sugar*
*1 egg*
*2 cups self-rising flour*
*½ teaspoon salt*
*1 cup milk*
*1 teaspoon vanilla*
*2 cups huckleberries or blueberries*
*1 tablespoon flour*

Preheat oven to 350°. Mix together butter, sugar and egg and blend in flour and salt. Add milk and vanilla. Lightly coat berries with the tablespoon of flour, then add carefully to mixture. Bake in lightly greased pan for 40 minutes.

∩

## BANANA BREAD

*½ cup shortening*
*1 cup sugar*
*2 eggs, beaten*
*1 cup mashed ripe bananas*
*1 teaspoon lemon juice*
*2 cups sifted flour*
*3 teaspoons baking powder*
*½ teaspoon salt*
*1 cup chopped nuts*

Cream shortening and sugar together. Beat eggs until light. Press bananas through sieve and add lemon juice. Blend with creamed mixture. Sift flour, baking powder and salt together and mix quickly into banana mixture. Add nuts. Bake in a greased loaf pan at 375° for about 1¼ hours.

## BANANA NUT BREAD

⅓ cup shortening

⅔ cup sugar

3 eggs, beaten well

1 cup chopped banana

1¾ cups sifted flour

1 teaspoon baking soda

2 teaspoon cream of tartar

½ teaspoon salt

½ cup chopped nuts

Combine shortening and sugar and mix until creamy. Add eggs and banana and mix well. Sift all dry ingredients together and mix with banana combination and nuts. Pour batter into sprayed loaf pan. Bake at 350° for 1 hour. (Lisa Higgins)

Ω

## AUNT FAY'S CINNAMON BREAD
**1920's Recipe**

4 teaspoons baking powder

½ teaspoon salt

2 cups wheat flour

1 egg

¾ cup milk

3 tablespoons butter, melted

½ cup sugar

Add baking powder and salt to the flour. Break the egg into a mixing bowl and beat well. Add the milk, sugar and butter to the egg mixture and stir. Pour the dry ingredients into egg mixture. Beat until well blended. Pour into greased pans and bake at 400° for 20 minutes.

> **Rumor travels faster, but don't stay put as long as truth.**
> —*Will Rogers*

## JACKIE DREW
## GLAZED PEANUT BREAD

*1 ½ cups hot milk*
*¾ cups peanut butter*
*¾ cups packed brown sugar*
*2 eggs*
*2 cups flour*
*4 teaspoons baking powder*
*¼ teaspoon salt*
*¾ cup chopped peanuts*

In a large mixing bowl slowly pour hot milk over peanut butter, mixing at low speed until blended. Add brown sugar and eggs. Stir together the flour, baking powder and salt. Add to peanut butter mixture. Beat at medium speed to moisten flour, about 15 seconds. Stir in peanuts and spoon batter into a greased 8½ x 4½-inch loaf pan. Bake at 325° for 1 hour or until done. Brush on glaze.

**Glaze:**

*¼ cup sugar*
*4 teaspoons orange juice*

Combine sugar and orange juice and mix well. Brush on hot bread and cool.

## NUT BREAD

4 teaspoons baking powder
¾ teaspoon baking soda
1 teaspoon salt
1 egg, beaten
1 ¼ cups sour milk
½ cup sugar
3 cups wheat flour
1 cup chopped walnuts

Sift flour, baking powder, baking soda and salt together. Add sour milk and sugar to the beaten egg and mix. Add dry ingredients into egg mixture. Add chopped nuts. Beat until well mixed. Bake at 325° for 1 hour or until it is done when tested. Use dates or raisins instead of walnuts as variation.

∩

## BROCCOLI BREAD

1 package cornbread mix
½ cup melted butter
½ cup cottage cheese
1 small onion, finely chopped
2 eggs, beaten
1 teaspoon salt
1 small package frozen broccoli

Mix all ingredients and pour into a sprayed 9 x 13-inch pan. Bake at 400° for 35 minutes.

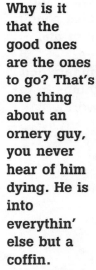

**Why is it that the good ones are the ones to go? That's one thing about an ornery guy, you never hear of him dying. He is into everythin' else but a coffin.**

—Will Rogers

[279]

## OKLAHOMA CORNBREAD

*1½ cups cornmeal*
*½ cup flour*
*1 teaspoon salt*
*1 teaspoon baking powder*
*½ teaspoon baking soda*
*2 eggs, beaten*
*1 cup buttermilk*
*3 tablespoons oil*

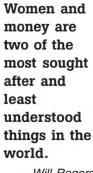

**Women and money are two of the most sought after and least understood things in the world.**

*—Will Rogers*

Preheat oven to 400°. Sift dry ingredients into a bowl. Add eggs and buttermilk and stir just enough to blend. Heat oil in a 9-inch skillet, allowing skillet to be completely greased. Pour excess hot oil into cornbread batter. Pour batter into hot skillet and bake for 25 minutes or until golden brown

∩

## GRANDMA'S 1920s CORNBREAD

*2 eggs*
*1½ cups sour milk*
*3 tablespoons shortening*
*³⁄₈ cup sugar*
*1½ cups corn meal*
*1½ cups flour*
*¾ teaspoon baking soda*
*4 teaspoons baking powder*
*1½ teaspoons salt*

Mix eggs, milk, shortening and sugar and beat well. Add all remaining ingredients and mix well. Grease a 9 x 9-inch square baking pan. Bake at 375° until golden brown.

## SOUTHERN CORN BREAD

*1½ cups scalded milk*
*1½ cups white cornmeal*
*1 teaspoon salt*
*2 tablespoons shortening*
*2½ teaspoons baking powder*
*1 egg yolk*
*1 egg white, beaten stiffly*

Mix milk and cornmeal and stir in salt and shortening. Cool. Add baking powder and egg yolk and mix well. Fold in stiffly beaten egg white. Pour into greased pan and bake at 400° for 20 minutes.

## GENE'S CORNBREAD

*1 egg*
*1¼ cups milk*
*1 stick margarine*
*1½ cups self-rising cornmeal*

Mix egg and milk together. Melt margarine in a 9- or 10-inch cast iron skillet in oven while preheating oven to 425°. Pour one-half melted margarine into milk and egg mixture, return skillet to oven and get margarine hot. Add cornmeal to milk, egg and margarine mixture. Do not over mix. More milk may be added if needed to make it pour easily. Pour into hot skillet with hot margarine. When margarine comes up the sides of skillet, spoon over top of mixture. Bake 30 to 40 minutes or until golden brown. (Gene McFall)

## OUT WEST CORNBREAD

*1 cup cornmeal*
*¼ cup flour*
*1 teaspoon salt*
*1 ½ cups boiling water*
*Pinch baking soda*
*Oil*

Combine dry ingredients. Pour boiling water over mixture and stir until moistened. Let cool and make into small patties. Fry in oil until golden brown.

Ω

## COWPOKE CORNBREAD

*1 ½ cups white cornmeal*
*½ tablespoon salt*
*¾ cup boiling water*
*Bacon grease*

Mix cornmeal and salt and pour in boiling water, heating constantly. Drop by tablespoonful in hot bacon grease, turn once. Cook until golden brown.

Ω

## FRIED CORNBREAD

*1 cup cornmeal*
*½ teaspoon baking soda*
*½ teaspoon salt*
*2 eggs, beaten*
*1 ¼ cups buttermilk*
*2 teaspoons shortening*

Sift cornmeal, soda and salt together. Add beaten eggs, then buttermilk. Beat until smooth. Dip a tablespoon of batter onto greased, hot griddle or skillet. Let brown, then turn and brown on other side.

## BLACK-EYE CORNBREAD

*1 pound ground beef, browned, drained*
*1 cup cornmeal*
*½ cup all-purpose flour*
*¾ cup cream style corn*
*1 cup black-eyed peas, cooked or*
  *canned, drained*
*1 onion, chopped*
*½ cup vegetable oil*
*1 cup buttermilk*
*2 eggs, beaten*
*2 cups shredded cheddar cheese*

**A country is known by its strength, and a man by his checkbook.**
—*Will Rogers*

Preheat oven to 350°. Combine all ingredients in a large bowl, mixing well. Pour into a greased 13 x 9-inch baking pan. Bake for 40-45 minutes or until bread is golden brown. Makes 8 to 10 servings.

## DROP SPOON ROLLS

*1 package dry yeast*
*2 cups warm water*
*¾ cup butter, melted*
*¼ cup sugar*
*1 egg, beaten*
*4 cups self-rising flour*

In a large bowl, place yeast in 2 cups warm water and add melted butter; gradually add sugar and stir. Add beaten egg to dissolved yeast mixture, then flour and stir until thoroughly mixed. Let stand 30 minutes. Drop by spoonfuls into well greased 2½-inch muffin tins and bake at 400° for about 20 minutes. Makes 2 dozen. (Linda Burgett)

## REFRIGERATOR ROLLS

¾ cup shortening
1 cup boiling water
2 eggs, beaten
¾ cup sugar
2 teaspoons salt
1 cup cold water
2 cakes yeast
½ cup lukewarm water
7½ cups sifted flour

Combine shortening and boiling water and stir until shortening is melted. Combine eggs, sugar and salt and beat in cold water. Soften yeast in lukewarm water. Combine the 3 mixtures and slowly add flour. Cover and chill overnight. Shape into rolls and let rise. Bake at 425° until golden brown. Makes 36.

Ω

## EASY NO-KNEAD ROLLS

2 packages dry yeast
2 cups warm water
½ cup sugar
2 teaspoons salt
½ cup oil
2 eggs, beaten
6½ cups flour

Dissolve yeast in warm water in large bowl. Add sugar, salt, oil and eggs; mix well. Add flour gradually and mix well. Place in greased bowl and chill, covered for 2 hours. Shape into rolls. Place on greased baking sheet. Let rise for 1½ to 2 hours or until doubled in bulk. Bake at 375° for 15 to 20 minutes. May store dough in refrigerator for 5 days. Makes 36 rolls.

## HOMEMADE CINNAMON ROLLS

1 ¼ cups milk
¼ cup shortening
1 ½ teaspoons salt
2 packages yeast
3 eggs, slightly beaten
4 ½ cups flour
1 cup melted butter, divided
1 ⅓ cups sugar, divided
3 tablespoons cinnamon

Scald milk; add shortening and salt. Cook to luke-warm. Add yeast and eggs. Blend in flour and knead until satiny. Let rise until double in size; then punch down. Let rise again and roll out. Brush with ⅔ melted butter. Mix 1 cup sugar and cinnamon and spread onto dough. Roll and cut into 1-inch slices. Let rise. Bake at 375° for 20 to 25 minutes. Frost with remaining sugar and melted butter while warm.(Debbie Davis)

∩

## QUICK SEEDED ROLLS

1 (8-ounce package) brown and serve rolls
2 tablespoons margarine or butter, melted
¼ teaspoon salt
½ teaspoon sesame seeds, poppy seeds or
    caraway seeds

Place rolls on ungreased cookie sheet and brush tops with margarine. Sprinkle with onion salt and sesame seeds. Bake as directed on package.

**Everything the Lord has a hand in is going great, but the minute you notice anything that is in any way under the supervision of man, why it's cockeyed.**
—Will Rogers

## SURPRISE MARSHMALLOW ROLLS

*6 triangle shaped crescent roll dough*
*1¼ teaspoons cinnamon*
*2½ tablespoons sugar*
*6 large marshmallows*
*3 tablespoons margarine or butter, melted*

Preheat oven to 375°. Mix cinnamon and sugar together. Dip each marshmallow in melted butter and then in cinnamon and sugar mixture. Roll crescent dough around dipped marshmallows, completely covering it. Pinch ends to seal, dip in butter and place in a muffin tin. When muffin tin is full, sprinkle sugar and cinnamon on top of rolls. Place a large piece of aluminum foil under muffin tins when baking. Bake for 10 to 15 minutes. (Ann Heston)

Ω

## APPLE ROLLS

*2 cups flour*
*3 tablespoons baking powder*
*¾ cup milk*
*½ teaspoon salt*
*1 egg*
*2 tablespoons sugar*
*¾ teaspoon cinnamon, divided*
*3 tablespoons butter*
*7 medium apples, peeled and sliced*
*1½ cups packed brown sugar*
*¾ cup water*

Mix flour, baking powder, milk, salt and egg. Turn out on floured board like a jellyroll. Spread dough with butter and sprinkle with mixture of sugar and cinnamon. Now arrange apples on dough and roll. Cut in 1-inch pieces and set in pan of brown sugar and water. Bake at 375° until golden brown.

## CATTLE DRIVE HUSH PUPPIES

2¼ cups self-rising cornmeal
3 tablespoons self-rising flour
1 tablespoon finely chopped onion
1 egg
1 cup milk or water
Oil

Combine cornmeal, flour and onion, add egg and gradually beat in milk or water. Drop from a spoon into hot oil where fish was fried. Fry until golden brown and drain on paper towels. Makes 16.

∩

## OKLAHOMA SWEET POTATO BISCUITS

2 cups flour
⅔ cup sugar
1½ teaspoons salt
2 tablespoons baking powder
¼ cup shortening
2 cups mashed, cooked sweet potatoes
Milk
Flour

Sift flour, sugar, salt and baking powder together and cut in shortening until it resembles oatmeal. Stir in sweet potatoes. Add milk gradually to form a soft dough. Turn on a lightly floured board and knead lightly. Pat out to ½ inch thickness, then cut out biscuits with biscuit cutter or small glass. Place on a greased cookie sheet and bake at 475° for 12 to 15 minutes.

When Congress makes a joke it's a law. And when they make a law it's a joke.
—Will Rogers

## OLD-TIME BISCUITS

*2 cups flour*
*1 teaspoon salt*
*4 teaspoons baking soda*
*4 tablespoons shortening*
*¾ cup milk*
*Flour*

Preheat oven to 450°. Sift flour, salt and baking powder into a mixing bowl. Cut shortening into dry mixture until crumbly and add milk, just enough to make a soft dough. Turn out dough on slightly floured board and knead gently to ½ inch thick. Bake until lightly browned, about 12 minutes. (Joan Franklin)

**It's not what you pay a man but what he costs you that counts.**

—Will Rogers

Ω

## DROP BISCUITS

*2 cups flour*
*4 teaspoons baking powder*
*2 teaspoons sugar*
*½ teaspoon salt*
*½ teaspoon cream of tartar*
*½ cup shortening*
*1 cup milk*

Sift flour, baking powder, sugar, salt and cream of tartar, then add shortening. Mix well. Add milk and stir well. Drop by spoonful on ungreased cookie sheet. Bake at 350° until lightly browned, about 10-15 minutes.

## CHEESE NIBBLE BISCUITS

1 (10-count) package refrigerated biscuits
3 tablespoons butter, melted
½ teaspoon chili powder
½ cup shredded cheddar cheese
¼ cup chopped jalapeno peppers

Cut biscuits into quarters and combine butter and chili powder in 9-inch pie plate. Place biscuit pieces in pie plate and toss to coat each piece with butter mixture. Sprinkle cheese and peppers on top. Bake at 350° until brown, about 15 minutes.

∩

## CAN'T RESIST MUFFINS

1½ cups old-fashioned rolled oats
1 cup flour
½ cup raisins
½ cup chopped walnuts
⅓ cup firmly packed brown sugar
1 tablespoon baking powder
¾ teaspoon salt
⅔ cup milk
⅓ cup oil
1 large egg, beaten
¼ cup honey

Preheat oven to 400°. Grease or line 12 standard size muffin pan with paper cups. In a large bowl, stir together oats, flour, raisins, nuts, brown sugar, baking powder and salt. In a separate bowl, stir together milk, oil, beaten egg and honey. Stir the milk mixture into the oat mixture just until the dry ingredients are moistened. Fill muffin cups about ⅔ full. Bake 15 to 18 minutes until muffins turn golden brown. Serve hot with butter or honey. Makes 12 muffins.

## SALLY LUNN MUFFINS

*2 cups sifted flour*
*3 teaspoons baking powder*
*½ teaspoon salt*
*1 egg, beaten*
*1 cup milk*
*½ cup shortening*
*¼ cup sugar*

Sift flour with baking powder and salt. Combine egg and milk. Cream shortening and sugar together and add flour mixture alternately with liquid mixture. Place batter in greased loaf pan or muffin pan and bake at 375° for 30 minutes. Makes 1 loaf or 12 muffins.

Ω

## TASTY SAUSAGE MUFFINS

*½ pound pork sausage*
*Butter*
*2 cups flour*
*1 tablespoon baking powder*
*¼ teaspoon salt*
*2 tablespoons sugar*
*1 egg, beaten*
*1 cup milk*
*½ cup shredded cheese*

Cook sausage over medium heat until done and drain and crumble, reserving drippings. Add butter to drippings to measure ¼ cup. Set sausage and drippings aside. Mix flour, baking powder, salt and sugar in medium bowl. Mix egg, milk and ¼ cup of drippings and stir well. Add to dry mixture and stir until moistened. Stir in sausage and cheese, spoon into muffin cups and fill ¾ full. Bake at 375° for 18 minutes.

## LOG CABIN HONEY MUFFINS

*1½ cups flour*
*2 teaspoons baking powder*
*¼ teaspoon salt*
*1 tablespoon sugar*
*1 egg, beaten*
*⅔ cup milk*
*3 tablespoons melted shortening*

Sift together flour, baking powder, salt and sugar into a mixing bowl. Add milk, egg and melted shortening. Stir to mix. Add all at one time to flour mixture in bowl. Stir only until flour is well-moistened. Batter may look a bit lumpy. Spoon batter into muffin pans on top of honey-coconut mixture, below. Fill each cup ⅔ full. Bake at 400° for 25 to 30 minutes. When done, loosen edges of muffins with spatula or knife tip and turn out at once. Drizzle any remaining honey mixture in pan over muffins.

∩

## HONEY-COCONUT MIXTURE

*⅓ cup sugar*
*¼ cup honey*
*2 tablespoons shortening*
*¼ cup coconut, divided*

Combine sugar, honey and shortening in a small saucepan. Bring to boil slowly, stirring constantly. Remove from heat. Measure 2 teaspoons of this syrup into each muffin cup. Sprinkle 1 teaspoon coconut into each cup on top of honey mixture. Set aside while preparing batter.

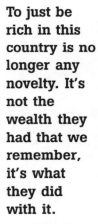

**To just be rich in this country is no longer any novelty. It's not the wealth they had that we remember, it's what they did with it.**

—*Will Rogers*

## 1920s TWIN MOUNTAIN MUFFINS
### Will Rogers Memorial Carolyn Deffenbaugh

*½ cup sugar*
*½ cup margarine, softened*
*2 eggs*
*1 ½ cups milk*
*4 cups flour*
*6 teaspoons baking powder*
*1 teaspoon salt*

Preheat oven to 350°. Cream sugar and margarine together; add eggs, milk, flour, baking powder and salt. Bake in greased muffin tins for 25 minutes. Makes 18 muffins.

## SOPAIPILLAS

*4 cups flour*
*1 ¼ teaspoons salt*
*3 teaspoons baking powder*
*3 tablespoons sugar*
*1 ¼ cups milk*
*2 tablespoons shortening*
*Flour*
*Oil for deep frying*

Sift the flour and measure it; sift again with salt, baking powder and sugar. Cut in the shortening and milk to make a soft dough just firm enough to roll. Place in bowl and cover. Let stand 25 minutes. Then roll to a quarter-inch thickness on a lightly floured board and cut into diamonds. Heat about 1 inch of oil in a frying pan to about 380° and remove dough when both sides are golden brown.

## FLOUR TORTILLAS

*2 cups flour*
*1½ teaspoons salt*
*1 teaspoon baking powder*
*4 tablespoons shortening*
*⅔ cup warm water*
*Flour*

Sift flour, salt and baking powder and cut in shortening as you do for pie crusts. Slowly add warm water as you blend all ingredients only long enough to form a firm ball. Pinch off dough in pieces the size of a lemon, form into ball and roll out in thin circles on floured board. Cook on hot griddle or in frying pan with no oil. When tortilla begins to brown, turn and cook on other side. Spread them out ˇtil they are only warm.

**Big business sure got big, but it got big by selling its stocks and not by selling its products.**

—*Will Rogers*

∩

## COWBOY COFFEE CAKE

*2 (10 or 12-count) cans refrigerated biscuits*
*⅓ cup buttery flavored oil*
*⅓ cup packed brown sugar*
*⅓ cup chopped nuts*
*1 teaspoon cinnamon*

Overlap biscuits in 9-inch cake pan in a spiral fashion. Combine oil, brown sugar, nuts and cinnamon and spread over biscuits. Bake at 350° for 30 minutes. Makes 6 to 8 servings.

## HOMESTEAD WAFFLES

*2 cups sifted flour*
*1 tablespoon cornmeal*
*1 teaspoon baking soda*
*½ teaspoon salt*
*2 eggs, separated*
*2 cups sour cream*

Sift flour, cornmeal, baking soda and salt together. Beat yolks and add cream. Add sifted dry ingredients and mix well. Fold in stiffly beaten egg whites. Bake in hot waffle iron. Makes 6.

Ω

## KANSAS TWISTERS

*¼ cup shortening*
*1 cup sugar*
*2 eggs, beaten*
*3½ teaspoons baking powder*
*¼ teaspoon nutmeg*
*½ teaspoon salt*
*4 cups sifted flour, divided*
*1 cup milk*

Cream shortening. Add sugar, then beaten eggs, sift baking powder, nutmeg and salt with 1 cup of flour and add alternately with milk to first mixture. Add additional flour to make a dough stiff enough to handle. Toss on floured board, roll ½-inch thick and cut into strips. Twist and fry in deep oil at 365°. Drain and when cold, roll in confectioner's sugar. Makes 3 dozen.,

**It won't be no time til some woman will become so desperate politically and just lose all prospective of right and wrong and maybe go from bad to worse and finally wind up in the Senate.**

—*Will Rogers*

# COFFEE CAKE WITH CRUMB TOPPING

1 ½ cups sifted flour
½ cup sugar
2 teaspoons baking powder
½ teaspoon salt
1 egg
⅔ cup milk
3 tablespoons shortening

Sift flour, sugar, baking powder and salt together. Beat egg and add milk and shortening. Stir liquids into dry ingredients, mixing only enough to dampen all the flour. Pour into greased pan, sprinkle with crumb topping and bake at 425° for 25 minutes.

### Crumb Topping:

2 tablespoons butter
2 tablespoons sugar
¼ cup sifted flour
¼ cup dry breadcrumbs
½ teaspoon cinnamon

Cream butter and sugar together. Add flour, breadcrumbs and cinnamon. Mix to consistency of coarse crumbs and sprinkle over coffee-cake batter before baking.

## GOLDEN BREADSTICKS

⅓ cup margarine or butter
1½ cups buttermilk baking mix
⅓ cup milk
Salt

Preheat oven to 450°. Heat butter in 13 x 9 x 2-inch baking pan in oven until melted. Mix baking mix and milk until soft dough forms. Smooth dough into ball on floured board and knead 5 times. Roll into rectangle, 6 x 4 inches. Cut lengthwise into 8 strips. Dip each strip into melted butter, coating all sides and place in pan. Sprinkle with salt. Bake until golden brown, 10 to 12 minutes. Makes 8 sticks.

∩

## JOHNNY CAKE

2 cups cornmeal
1½ teaspoons salt
1 teaspoon baking soda
2 tablespoons sugar
2 cups sour milk
2 eggs, beaten
2 tablespoons melted shortening

Sift dry ingredients together and add milk, eggs and shortening. Mix well. Pour into greased pan and bake at 400°. Makes 1 loaf.

## APPLE FLAPJACKS

1 tablespoon shortening
1 teaspoon sugar
2 eggs, beaten
1½ cups sifted flour
1 teaspoon baking powder
½ teaspoon cinnamon
1 cup chopped apples
1 cup milk

Cream shortening and sugar, add beaten eggs and flour sifted with baking powder and cinnamon. Add chopped apples and milk gradually to make a medium batter. Bake on a griddle for ordinary pancakes. Cooked apples may be used in batter in the same way. Makes 16. (Jean Williams)

∩

## QUICK DOUGHNUTS

1 package canned refrigerator biscuits
Oil
3 tablespoons sugar
1½ teaspoons cinnamon

Make doughnuts by cutting out the centers of each biscuit. Heat oil in deep fat fryer or skillet. Gently drop doughnut in hot oil and cook until lightly brown. Turn and brown second side. Remove from skillet. Drain on paper towels. Roll in cinnamon/sugar mixture. (Pat Howell)

I think the best insurance in the world against another war is to take care of the boys who fought in the last one. You may want to use them again.

—Will Rogers

## SPOON IN DOUGHNUTS

*3 eggs*
*1 cup sugar*
*1 cup milk*
*½ teaspoon salt*
*2 teaspoons baking powder*
*3 cups flour*
*2 tablespoons melted shortening*
*Sugar*

Beat eggs and add sugar and milk. Sift salt, baking powder and flour together and add to liquid. Beat thoroughly and add melted shortening. Add more flour to make a batter stiff enough to hold a spoon in standing position. Drop by spoonful into deep oil at 365°. Remove when brown and drain on paper towels. Roll in sugar. Makes 3 dozen. (Diane Reasoner)

## OLD-TIMER'S PANCAKES

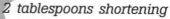

*2 tablespoons shortening*
*1 egg, beaten*
*1 ¼ cups buttermilk*
*½ teaspoon baking soda*
*1 ¼ cups flour*
*1 teaspoon sugar*
*1 teaspoon baking powder*
*½ teaspoon salt*

Heat griddle with a little shortening. Combine all ingredients and beat until smooth. Bake on griddle over medium high heat.

## JAMES WHITMORE'S COFFEE CAN BREAD

2 (1-pound) coffee cans, empty
4 cups all-purpose flour, divided
1 package dry yeast
½ cup butter
½ cup water
½ cup milk
¼ cup sugar
1 teaspoon salt
2 eggs, slightly beaten

Coat insides of two 1-pound coffee cans with small amounts of cooking oil. In a large bowl, mix 2 cups flour and yeast together. In a saucepan, stir together butter, water, milk, sugar and salt over low heat until butter melts. Cook 5 minutes. Add to flour and yeast. Mix in remaining 2 cups flour and eggs. Dough will be stiff. Turn onto a lightly floured board and knead until dough is smooth and elastic. Divide dough in half and place in prepared coffee cans. Cover with plastic lids and let rise in warm place until dough is 1 inch from top of can. Preheat oven to 375°. Remove plastic lids and bake 35 minutes. Remove from cans and let cool.

**We're all ignorant, only on different subjects.**
—*Will Rogers*

## QUICKIE BEER BREAD
**Will Rogers Memorial Carolyn Deffenbaugh**

3 cups self-rising flour
2 tablespoons sugar
1 (12-ounce) can beer
Butter, softened

In a large bowl, mix flour, sugar and beer. Blend with mixer and pour into greased loaf pan. Bake at 350° for 55 minutes. Remove from oven, brush top of loaf with soft butter and return to oven for 5 minutes.

# BIBLIOGRAPHY

Ayres, Alex. *Wit and Wisdom of Will Rogers.* Penguin Books, New York, 1993.

Carter, Joseph H. *Never Met A Man I Didn't Like.* Avon Books, New York, 1991.

Collins, Reba. *Will Rogers Says.* Will Rogers Heritage Press, Claremore OK, 1988.

*Will Rogers and Wiley Post in Alaska.* Will Rogers Heritage Press, Claremore, OK, 1984.

Ketchum, Richard M. *Will Rogers, His Life and Times.* American Heritage Publishing, New York, 1973.

Love, Paula McSpadden. *The Will Rogers Book.* Bobbs-Merrill, Inc., 1961, Texian Press, Waco, 1972.

Matthews, Wendell. *Will Rogers: The Man and His Humor.* Glenheath Publishers, Racine, WS, 1991.

McFall, Gene. *Witty World of Will Rogers.* Claremore, OK, 1999.

Payne, William H. and Lyons, Jake G. *Folks Say of Will Rogers: A Memorial Anecdotage.* G. P. Putnam's & Sons, New York, 1936.

Rogers, Betty. *Will Rogers: His Wife's Story.* Bobbs-Merrill Co., Inc., 1941, University of Oklahoma Press, 1979.

Sterling, Bryan B. *The Best of Will Rogers.* Crown Publishers, New York, 1979.

*The Will Rogers Scrapbook.* Grossett and Cunlap, New York, 1976.

Sterling, Bryan B. and Frances N. *Will Rogers in Hollywood.* Crown Publishers, New York, 1984.

*Will Rogers and Wiley Post: Death at Barrow.* M. Evans and Co., New York, 1993.

Wilson, Leland. *The Will Rogers Touch.* Brethren Press, Elgin, IL, 1978.

*Will Rogers Memorial and Birthplace, A Pictoral Tribute to an American Legend.* Will Rogers Heritage Trust, 1996.

# INDEX

# M

# N

# O

# P

# Cookbooks
# published by
# Cookbook Resources

The Four Ingredient Cookbook

•

Mother's Recipes

•

Recipe Keepsakes

•

Kitchen Keepsakes & More Kitchen Keepsakes

•

Cookin' With Will Rogers

•

Fresh Ideas For Vegetable Cooking

•

Homecoming

•

Mealtimes and Memories

•

Cookbook 25 Years

•

Texas Longhorn Cookbook

•

Little Taste of Texas

•

Leaving Home

Please send _____ copies of *Cookin' with Will Rogers*

@ $19.95 (U.S.) each  $_____

Plus postage and handling @ $3.50 each  $_____

Texas residents add sales tax @ $1.45 each  $_____

Check or Credit Card (Canada-credit card only) TOTAL  $_____

Charge to my: ☐ Master Card or ☐ Visa Card

Account # _____

Expiration Date _____

Signature _____

**MAIL TO:**
**Cookbook Resources**
**541 Doubletree Drive**
**Highland Village, Texas 75077**
**972-317-0245**

Name_____

Address _____

City _____ State _____ Zip _____

Phone (day) _____ (night) _____

— — — — — — — — — — — — — — — — — — — — — — — —

Please send _____ copies of *Cookin' with Will Rogers*

@ $19.95 (U.S.) each  $_____

Plus postage and handling @ $3.50 each  $_____

Texas residents add sales tax @ $1.45 each  $_____

Check or Credit Card (Canada-credit card only) TOTAL  $_____

Charge to my: ☐ Master Card or ☐ Visa Card

Account # _____

Expiration Date _____

Signature _____

**MAIL TO:**
**Cookbook Resources**
**541 Doubletree Drive**
**Highland Village, Texas 75077**
**972-317-0245**

Name_____

Address _____

City _____ State _____ Zip _____

Phone (day) _____ (night) _____

**GENE MCFALL** is nationally acclaimed for his portrayal of Will Rogers in his one-man show, *Witty World of Will Rogers.* He has appeared as the cowboy/humorist/philosopher in 45 states and around the world since 1982. The Will Rogers Memorial and the Rogers family say that Gene does the most authentic presentation of keeping this great American's memory alive. His performance depicts Will as he appeared on his lecture circuit in 1935. Everything he says in the show is taken directly from Will Rogers' writings or radio broadcasts, and are as applicable today as when he said them. Gene adapts his show to whatever situation he is playing: theatres, concerts, art series, conventions or meetings.

1-800-673-0768